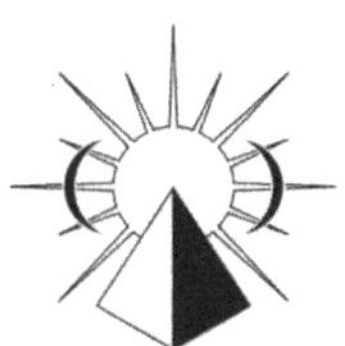

2026

The Precession of Sovereignty

The Future of Northern Civilization

Alexander J. Ziatyk

Table of Contents

"In the Middle Ages, an unbeliever was
regarded as a madman…
so repulsive that he was delivered to the stake.
…
In our time,
A subject who declared himself independent
from the State,
who refused to pay taxes, to render military
service,
and to recognize authority,
in short, to be his own government, would,
as unbelievers in the Middle Ages,
be declared insane,
but, instead of being burnt at the stake,
would either be forced to submit to the lawful
authorities
or be expelled from his country.
He might be transported to other territories,
where also he would be reduced to submission
or expelled."

- Konstantin Pobedonostsev[1]

***

"The pendulum swings not smoothly but violently:
tribal anarchy breeds longing for order,
and authoritarian order eventually generates the discontent
that drives fragmentation again."

- Mike Maxwell[2]

***

"Every accumulation ends in dissipation;
every rise ends in a fall;
every union ends in separation;
and life ends in death."

- The Agni Purana[3]

I

<u>The Ordering of Culture</u>

An elite ruling class requires authority. Authority requires sovereignty and sovereignty requires legitimacy. Legitimacy rests on the willingness of the masses to be ruled by an elite minority. This is the rotating wheel of power. Any elite who loses legitimacy must regain it or be crushed by the wheel as sovereignty moves to another central elite cadre (re-centralization) or to decentralized smaller elite units (fragmentation.)

Sovereignty always remains within an elite minority, whether in a universal imperium, a republic, a tribal clan or any other social configuration. The masses never have sovereignty. It is delusional to believe that the so-called "people" ever have power. They never have, and as long as they remain plural in their ethnoses, beliefs, ideas, desires and goals, they never will. It is not possible for large bodies of people to have power due to the fact that power prefers concentration and organization and diffuses itself amongst numbers of individuals as if there is only so much in existence; an inexhaustible supply, unlimited in depth but limited in breadth, expressing itself more profoundly and effectively the fewer people who possess it. Power, like an intelligent spiritual organism, selects individuals through whom it will express itself. This selection can be called charisma.

The manifest particularities of the expression of power – ideologies, laws, religions, cultures, wars, peacetime activities, division of labor, aesthetics, economics, etc. – are of no consequence to the fulfillment of the power impulse. All it desires, if it can be said to desire anything, is to combat the flattening, leveling and diffusive effects of entropy. It brings energy, vitality and order to what would otherwise be chaotic diffusion and decadence. It prefers quality over quantity. When the elite begin to prefer quantity over quality, legitimacy and therefore authority are lost and power will find new instruments through whom to express itself.

Power is generated either by the capacity and willingness to monopolize the commission of violence or the capacity to persuade others to refrain from committing violence. Possessing power allows for the creation of ideology – the imaginal ocean in which the human fish swim. Ideology allows for the enacting of laws, and law creates, guides and alters culture. This hierarchy of statecraft is an immutable iron law of human reality. Charisma begets persuasion. Persuasion begets a monopoly on violence. Monopoly on violence begets power. Power begets ideology.

Ideology begets law. Law begets culture. The quality of the culture produced in this way begets either legitimacy or illegitimacy for the governing elite and determines whether or not they will gain or maintain sovereignty. Should the governing elite have the approval of the masses, they are legitimate and may rule with very little coercion or repression. Should they not have the approval of the masses, they are illegitimate and will either lose sovereignty eventually or resort to coercion and repression that must increase in severity over time, as coercion and repression undermine their legitimacy even further. There is no changing this order of operations. Those who misunderstand this inevitably fail.

Remember, and remember well: cultures do not create laws. Laws create culture. And it is the governing elite who create laws, therefore; the creation of new or altered cultures is in the hands of the governing elite. The culture does not produce the elite. The elite produce the culture.

The transcendent spiritual impulses of charisma and power produce the elite either by selection and incarnation or by an individual wresting this chrism from the spiritual world through sheer will and accomplishment. Today, only the non-governing elite are selected in this way as the governing elite are not elite (e.g. "aristocratic") at all considering that they achieve their governing status through treachery, finance, and bureaucratic maneuvering.

To argue against this spiritual anointment of the elite is to invite failure, decadence, corruption and dissolution; it is to argue for the mass formation, materialistic, evolutionary theory of history which has proven to be a distortion and a falsehood resulting in the opening of the flood gates for hedonism, cynicism, tyranny, and decay. Higher things (the elite) do not originate from lower things (the culture.) Higher things create and govern lower things as per the cosmic spiritual hierarchy. In much the same way, those who are spiritually inclined understand that consciousness produces the brain, the brain does not produce consciousness. The brain receives and is governed by the higher spiritual intelligence. The ordering of any given society follows suit.

Human beings are spiritual beings incarnate in various quality. In a healthy and normal society, the highest spiritual humans are the elite, and they have much legitimacy, being endowed with incorruptible senses of honor and justice, they are generally well-liked by the masses. They are known as The Aristocracy. However, in dark ages, times of evil, decadence, spiritual ignorance and corruption, spiritually lower specimens of the human stock using coercive, vain and deceitful tactics may gain a relative monopoly on violence and thereby secure power for themselves and in so doing, produce ideologies, laws and cultures in their image. The onset and precession of such ages is a mystery and they are a great sadness and difficulty for people seeing as they may last millennia. But as sure as the spring follows winter and autumn follows summer, so too do better ages follow the worse, and worse follow the better.

This cyclical fact betrays a secret of good governance. It is not the system of government which constitutes the important factor in the attempt to achieve justice, prosperity, security, freedom and wellbeing for a people. Any system of government may produce these results so long as the elite minority are of the highest quality human beings, of noble character, incorruptible dignity and superior wisdom. Any system of government may produce terrible results if the elite minority are of low quality spirit, being base, greedy, vain, selfish, ignorant, unwise, and in lack of self-awareness and self-control, being dominated by their animalistic urges and emotional instabilities. Autarchy, Monarchy, Fascism, Tribal Chiefdom, Republicanism, and a number of other forms, both more primitive and more complex, may be excellent or terrible not because of their inherent natures or infrastructure, but because of the people at the helm. Human greatness and human shortcomings are the primary factors.

Although, there must be special consideration of the fact that democracy, including its communist and libertarian manifestations, cannot be said to be a system of government, and therefore must be excluded from the selection by the elite minority in their choice for which system they wish to implement, seeing that sovereignty and power cannot rightly lie within the hands of the masses of people. In truth, democracy is nothing other than plutocracy (rule by the financially wealthy) or its degenerate sister kleptocracy (rule by thieves) – both perversions of Republicanism. It is popular today to refer to this as "oligarchy," although I prefer the more accurate terms "kleptocracy" or "plutocracy," seeing that the greek root *oligos* simply means "the few." This of course describes the nature of every type of government and, therefore; every government is an oligarchy rendering the word essentially meaningless and useless for any form of structural criticism outside the echo chambers of raving anarchists, liberals and the immature New Right.

Democratic ideology (and its mutated offspring Communism and Libertarianism) allows for wealth to be extracted from the majority and concentrated in the hands of a minority while simultaneously undermining faith in noble persons (aristocrats) which enables this minority to ascend to elite status via finance and grasp the levers of power, generally by establishing their own institutions and organizations (in contradistinction to and competition with aristocratic establishments) which mobilize enormous resources to engage in the science of social engineering, thereby having a fundamental effect on the souls, minds, bodies, and therefore, behavior, goals and desires of the population without accountability to any body politik or code of conduct and often without much, or even any, awareness of such from the masses; let alone legal recourse should the masses become cognizant of these abuses, seeing as the kleptocrats write the laws in such societies and are endemically protected. Their abuses, while maybe considered unethical, are usually legal, and should they be proven illegal, the courts will be bought or coerced through the web of connections established by the kleptocrats that they will suffer no penalty or hindrance to the continuation of their deleterious activities.

The existence of this power is then denied publicly and exercised secretly in order to maintain the democratic illusion that the people have power; in fact, the people of such societies generally believe so much that sovereignty resides within the masses that these levers of power grasped by the wealthy elite are viewed not as levers of power at all, but as simply the harmless and fundamental educational, intellectual, economic, cultural and charitable foundations and institutions necessary for a functioning democracy. This ignorance insures the kleptocrats' safety and their unregulated, unsupervised enjoyment of wealth and power to the detriment of everyone, including, inevitably and eventually, themselves.

Only those systems of government which do not pretend to the democratic delusion but openly and honestly rely on the judgment and actions of the elite minority can be included as possible foundations for good governance. Any so-called "systems of government" which deny the immutable principle of elite rule are abortive to the maintenance of justice, prosperity, security, freedom and wellbeing of a people and therefore cannot be classified as systems of government and can only be classified as wishful thinking or outright deception. These are systems of quantity; not quality. They are concerned with quantity of votes (democracy) and quantity of money (finance); not quality of people (aristocracy) or quality of resources (industry.) No higher cultural activity can occur when secret kleptocracy and anarchic delusion are established in combination; and where they are found, it is always in combination, being the head and tail of a single serpent.

II

<u>Cultural Vitalism</u>

According to the great philosophic and religious traditions of every High Culture, whether we refer to Oswald Spengler, Rumi, shamans, medicine men, the Great Philosophers, the Bible, or the Vedas, cultures and their attendant civilizations are born, live and die just like any living organism and they develop, transform, express themselves and decay through the known life cycles and phases of organic entities, albeit on a somewhat grander scale. Francis Yockey believed that High Cultures were actual living spiritual organisms with desires and lifespans. This would go a long way in explaining the phenomena of multiple simultaneous inventions, spiritual teachings, and art form creations where various individuals without influence on one another create, think and act along the same lines at the same time. A High Culture, which we may imagine as an Oversoul or a National Deity, sends impulses into the human sphere in order to express itself through the human beings in its territory and under its influence who constitute its cellular structure and physical organs much the same way a person sends an impulse to their hand so they may grab a coffee mug, or the brain sends impulses to the stomach to govern the digestion of food. Human beings receive inspiration and direction from their cultural Oversoul and those individuals who are most open to these influences, understand them best and most effectively act on them become the great heroes, leaders, artists, sages, and inventors of a culture's history.

This theory is often referred to as Cultural Vitalism[4] and is the foundation for developing a strong historical sense, without which, it would be essentially impossible to understand one's place in history; carrying out responsible and conscientious actions therefore becomes highly unlikely. The lack of awareness of Cultural Vitalism and the commensurate lack of spiritual attunement to the Cultural Oversoul explains much of the decadent and foolhardy phenomena that can be witnessed throughout society: teachers teaching useless subjects and falsehoods, artists creating deplorable works, statesmen making unwise and selfish decisions, inventors being motivated by greed, would-be sages failing in their spiritual ascent and disseminating false teachings and distortions of truth to unprepared spiritual seekers, among many other such sadnesses and happenstances that I am sure you can imagine and witness on your own.

Such cultural distortions do not arise only during the decadent, dying, old-age, senile stage of a High Culture's lifetime; although the late stage certainly sees far more distortion than earlier more vital stages. Distortions may arise at any stage of a culture's history through people who lack awareness, attunement and historical sense. This is why a cultural elite is so important. They have the responsibility to be spiritually advanced individuals and must guide the masses who may lack spiritual development. An elite who lack this finely tuned and hard-won self-awareness, spiritual attunement and cultural sense will bring calamity and ruin to a civilization beyond the normal decay and decline of natural aging and death.

***

In this world, there exist different strata of life: the mineral, the plant, the animal, the man, the culture man, and the High Culture. Unlike these other materially incarnated entities, the High Culture is primarily a spiritual entity and is not subject to conventional perception. It is generally not something you can see with your eyes except in exalted states of mystical awareness or that has a conventional physical form except as seen in dreams, vivid moments of inspired imagination and certain paranormal encounters. But just as we cannot see the wind; we can however see and hear the leaves blowing in the trees or a curtain wafting by an open window or feel it cascading across our skin; we can infer the existence of the wind, and similarly, we can infer the existence of the High Culture.

We know through intuitive observation and experience what belongs to a particular culture and what does not. The different forms of art, music, spirituality, science, philosophy, architecture, eroticism, style of war, style of technics, education, society, law, style of imperialism, and so on, all have an internal cohesion that is usually more obvious to the cultural alien than to the members of the culture itself.

For example, over the last thousand years of history, the Africans, Arabs and Asians have seen the West as a cohesive unit known as the West. At the same time, Westerners were busy fighting intra-European wars, local kingdom against local kingdom, clan against clan. They saw keen differences amongst themselves: the Celts are different from the Saxons who are different from the Verangians who are different from the Slavs who are different from the Italians who are different from the Franks who are different from the Nords who are different from the Picts and so on. But to the cultural alien, they were all Westerners and their cultural forms mentioned above were intuitively coherent and based on similar, if not the same, mentality, worldview, and inner experience of reality. It is only very recently that we, as Westerners, have begun to view ourselves as a single unit in this same light, and there is a reason for that.

It is due to the natural life cycles and rhythms of the organism known as our High Culture. Like any organism, it goes through stages of birth, development, peak, aging, and death with all of their attendant attitude changes and goal reorientations. These attitude changes and goals, these historical missions that need to be fulfilled, are known as Spirits of the Ages. Each age that a High Culture passes through has a certain Spirit, a certain ethos or Culture Idea that urges us toward its fulfillment like a desire. In the current Age, we have a very keen sense of history which allows for deep pattern recognition resulting in cultural self-awareness, hence why we are beginning to see ourselves as the collective West. Less and less do individual Western nations matter to us as sovereign political units, but our feeling of sovereignty and politics is expanding to encompass all Western nations. Our differences melt away and our cultural and political unity takes center stage.

The Ages of a High Culture are generally as follows[4]:

- An early feudalistic period characterized by religious feeling and strong social cohesion. Although beginning as tribalistic and fragmented, it is not averse to centralization and eventually more or less coheres around some form of central authority. New spiritual ideas are generated in the psyches of great individuals. This period coincides with Sorokin's Ideational and Idealistic Truth System phases[15].

- Then, a period of critical spirituality, more individuality within religion, and the absolute state which pretends to democracy characterized by Rationalism, skepticism and atheism, placing the economy as the most important aspect and activity of human life. Politics becomes softened and feminized and replaced with legalism and moralism, and the pursuit of individual happiness is placed above all else, inspiring the systems of capitalism and communism. This period coincides with Sorokin's Sensate Truth System phase in which perceptions are rigidified and scientific materialistic ideas predominate. A general anti-spiritual mentality and sense of meaninglessness can very easily take hold of the population precipitating a crisis of degeneracy, cynicism and corruption. A dangerous and difficult transition phase is entered in which many High Cultures find their premature demise.

- This stage, if the transition is survived, is then followed by a period of the resurgence of Authority and deep re-envisioned spirituality characterized by penetrating universal wisdom hard-won by matured skepticism and with this comes a keen sense of history and pattern recognition and the correction of cultural errors. Think of a middle-aged man who reflects and recognizes the mistakes of his youth and corrects them with discipline and finality. The pursuit of individual happiness and the dogma of scientific materialism are seen as immature, feminine and foolish and activity becomes motivated instead by honor, duty, self-awareness and a sense of historical and spiritual necessity. This is a return to Sorokin's Ideational Truth System on a higher, more mature octave.

- And finally there is a period of Universal Imperium initiated by a type of Caesarism and characterized by absolute politics, after which, death from old age, the High Culture having fulfilled itself and spread its seed over the world like a great oak dropping its acorns and distributing the spiritually-dense nutrient rich compost of its decayed corpse over the world, giving vitality and strength to whichever young High Culture is beginning its life and takes into itself the rich spiritual fertilizer of the passed on High Culture. This is the peak of Sorokin's Idealistic Truth System phase - the spiritual idealism and seriousness of leaving behind an inspiring legacy utilizes the remaining stores of the aging High Culture's vitality.

As individual human beings, we are like the cells that make up the body of the High

Culture, and it sends impulses, inspiration, and impetus into us to think, act and speak in certain ways at certain times. The High Culture is our governing Oversoul, and we are the ones who act in the material world to fulfill the historical mission of our High Culture. A culture-bearing individual will attune him or herself to this Oversoul and act in accord with it. These people become the great artists, philosophers, inventors, statesmen, warriors, spiritual leaders and heroes of a culture who make the Spirit of the Age visible, palpable, tangible, manifest and actionable to the rest of the human beings within the culture letting them know which cultural, spiritual, technical and political directions are healthy to move in that will fulfill the High Culture's Idea of itself and which ideas and directions are distortions of the culture and are unhealthy and detrimental to the life of the High Culture. Other culture-bearing individuals are the people who enjoy, live by, appreciate and promulgate the works and ideas of the great and heroic personality types and are just as important and attuned as they are. They simply did not enter into creative or heroic fields because it was either unnecessary for the Culture Idea to fulfill itself or they have other cultural duties to fulfill like raising a family or living an appropriately healthy conventional life in support of the self-fulfillment of the High Culture according to the ideas made manifest by the works of the creative and heroic individuals.

This macrocosmic idea is reflected in the microcosm of an individual. As we age and go through life, we are exposed to ideas that are either from within ourselves or from outside, both helpful and harmful, and we intuitively search within ourselves to regulate our ideas and behaviors so that we act in accordance with what is truthful and authentic for ourselves, to fulfill our idea of ourselves. At least this is what healthy, self-aware, culture-bearing individuals do. Others who are not as self-aware, who are on auto-pilot, are susceptible to distorting ideas and will act in ways that harm themselves and others and work against the fulfillment of the culture Idea, against the Spirit of the Age. The extent to which you are self-aware is the extent to which you are aware of the High Culture. The extent to which you lack self-awareness, is the extent to which you are susceptible to the seductive ideas of distorters, aliens, and people who are operating from the ideas of a previous outgrown Spirit of a previous Age which is no longer beneficial but becomes harmful if it overstays its welcome, much like a sixty year old with the mentality of a twenty year old.

Now there are obviously two ways for a High Culture to die, just like any other organism. Firstly, of old age after self-fulfillment, or secondly, prematurely due to illness, hostility or accident. After the first type of death, the corpse of the High Culture is healthy and gives richness to the future of the world. After the second type of death, the remnants of the culture may possibly become pollutants and can cause malady and disease in a new High Culture. For just like material organisms, the spiritual organism of the High Culture can also suffer pathologies and diseases, but of course these are spiritual pathologies, not physical maladies. These pathologies are Culture-Parasitism, Culture-Retardation, and Culture-Distortion[4].

Culture-Parasitism is brought into the geographic and political territory of the High Culture by the alien, a person who belongs to a completely different culture. For each alien within the geographic territory of a High Culture, a person from the High Culture cannot be born. Culture-Parasitism is a one-to-one displacement of the population. If a million Africans are living in the heart of Europe, that means a million Europeans cannot be born. This is not to say that you should hate the alien or feel anger toward him, for real absolute politics has no place for petty emotionality. It is a simple statement of fact that a foreign entity inside of a host entity which does not assimilate to the host is by its very nature a parasite. This is not a derogatory statement. It is a simple truth. A person does not get angry at a tapeworm. They simply recognize it as a problem which needs a solution and they take steps toward the solution. There is no enmity, there is no animosity, nor is there any moralism here. It's just simple politics and self-preservation.

Culture-Retardation manifests in an organism when old, outmoded ways of thinking and acting overstay their welcome, when the Spirit of an old Age remains in the hearts and minds of some senile people well into the new Age and clashes with the principles and ideas of the new Spirit of the new Age. Our Western culture suffers greatly from this. The 18th century ideas of democracy and liberalism have long overstayed their welcome as the Spirit of the Age now is the resurgence of Authority. And the idea of capitalism invented by the British in the 19th century has overstayed its welcome as well, preventing us from moving into a more ethical and useful form of economics. Liberalism, democracy and capitalism were created by the Age of Rationalism, Skepticism and Economic Thinking which served us well for a time, but they do not serve us anymore and are causing serious Culture-Distortion which costs the physical and spiritual lives and wellbeing of untold millions of Westerners. The individuals of the 20th century who were manifesting the Spirit of the new Age (albeit in an imperfect tainted and contingent manner) trying to bring about the next natural development of the Western life cycles and rhythms were ruthlessly thwarted, misrepresented, destroyed, disenfranchised, used as controlled opposition and, in death, humiliated and ridiculed by the hate-filled, jealous, avaricious, power-hungry and terrified Culture-Parasites, Culture-Retards and Culture-Distorters.

Culture-Distortion comes from both Parasitism and Retardation. If Parasitism and Retardation are the cause of the disease, Distortion is the disease itself. When a cultural-alien lives within a High Culture not its own, they may gain benefit from a certain Spirit of a certain Age of that High Culture and wish to make that mode of activity permanent and prevent the development into a new Spirit of a new Age so that they may continuously benefit forever at the expense of the people of that High Culture. This is an acute form of Parasitism taken to the next level, exploiting the weaknesses of Culture-Retardation. Not only do they displace the High Culture's population, but they actively exploit it for their own gain, taking the ideas and wishes of Culture-Retards and surreptitiously enacting them as policy to artificially extend an old Age past its expiration date.

For example, imagine a race that had its own High Culture but failed to fulfill its historical mission. It met an untimely end before it could die of old age. This culture was at its life cycle stage of the ascendance of economic thinking – i.e: capitalism, communism, rationalism and democracy – at the moment of its untimely collapse caused by external circumstances or cultural disease. And so, this race in its condition of being an international diaspora is now permanently locked into this way of thinking and acting to the extent that they generally do not assimilate to the High Culture in which they currently live but remain tribally and ideologically cohesive with each other. The remnants and diaspora of a passed on High Culture tend to remain at the mode of activity they were in at the moment of its death if that death was caused by anything other than old age.

If they adopt the life cycles and rhythms of the new High Culture in which they live and totally assimilate to it, accepting their customs, language, traditions, economics, laws, manners, morality, and so on, they are no longer parasites; they are numbered amongst the High Culture's population and there is no problem and no more displacement. But to the extent that they love the economy and place the economy as the highest good and wealth acquisition as the purpose of life, they will use all of their will and resources to artificially keep a High Culture in its life cycle stage of economic thinking and rationalism so that they may continually benefit therefrom. This includes, but is not limited to, the use of propaganda, the infiltration and corruption of academia, the alteration of the historical record, lobbying and infiltration of the government and its attendant think tanks, embedding themselves in the legal system to protect themselves from scrutiny, domination and debasement of the financial system, and the coercion, demoralization, and demonizing of the race belonging to the High Culture.

A parasite such as this would not benefit from a resurgence of Authority which inherently eliminates the power and thrall of money. Authority places the economy at the bottom of the Pyramid of Society. The economy is simply a foundation for higher cultural activity and serves no other goal than to allow the fulfillment of the High Culture's historical mission. An Authoritarian age is concerned with culture, self-defense and spirituality, not wealth acquisition. Clearly, a capitalist or a communist or a rationalist or a liberal would not benefit from a resurgence of Authority. In fact, they will actively oppose this resurgence in order to preserve their own wealth and political power and their need for creature comforts and individual happiness, for they are indeed the natural enemies of Authority, Honor and Duty. Unscrupulous bankers, financiers, businessmen, kleptocrats, economists, liberals, parliamentarians and egalitarians despise monarchs, autocrats, charismatic dictators, and aristocratic culture-bearing personalities who would revoke their political access and power over the institutions and people of a society and place them as servants of those institutions and people, or simply eliminate their mediocre ideologies wholesale and demand that they act with Honor, Duty, Spiritual Awareness and Discipline.

This is the most difficult and dangerous transition in a High Culture's life cycles. Due to the fact that Culture-Distorters can easily ascend the social hierarchy in the era of rationalism, democracy, and economic-thinking using simple financial and bureaucratic tactics, they have vast resources at their disposal and have entrenched themselves into the fabric of civilization by establishing their own institutions and *sub rosa* networks. People in general are also very likely to become Culture-Retards in extremely large numbers in such an era because their animal nature is gratified by the ease with which they may collect money and ascend the hierarchy through bureaucracy and finance. This means that most people have become accustomed to the ideologies of liberalism and economics and will endeavor to maintain them as part of the culture. This transition is not a simple growth and development or change of mood as are the other types of transitions. This one is akin to identifying and rooting out diseases and parasites which are capable of defending themselves. Not only is the transition from Rationalism to Authority a treacherous and fundamentally transformative balancing act between

Collectivism and Individualism, it is also fraught with the conflict between Tradition and Innovation and the recognition of what a good worthy Tradition is versus an outmoded form of activity masquerading as Tradition. Discernment is also needed for recognizing a good worthy innovation from progressive, rationalistic nonsense.

For example, the American Constitution and similar European documents are products of the Age of Rationalism and Liberalism and serve almost no purpose today due to the fact that historical necessity and pattern recognition have disproven the dogmatic beliefs in equality, radical individualism and democracy. These were simply the peculiar religious tenets of a temporary mode of activity serving a particular purpose in our historical mission which has already been fulfilled. Radical individualism has turned us into an ocean of atoms in which people strive for sameness, equality, mediocrity and social acceptance and shun excellence and uniqueness. Belief in equality and democracy has left us open to attack from Culture-Parasites and Distorters who do not share our sense of compassion or tolerance but will exploit them and use them against us as weapons of guilt and ladders to power. It has also eliminated our ability to act heroically, for to be a hero means to stand out with excellence and uniqueness and take a strong stance against an enemy, but in a "democratic" society, there is no real enemy to defeat, there are only interest groups to out-vote and business rivals to sabotage; meanwhile, aristocratic counter-elite heroic and creative personalities are largely viewed as the "enemy" by the culturally retarded masses. The one who controls the media and academia controls the minds of the voters, and to point out this fact does not make you a hero in today's world, but an intolerant bigot who doesn't understand love and acceptance. These so-called "traditions" of constitutionalism, democracy, and equality are not traditions at all, but anachronisms from an earlier time which did not contain today's historical necessity of Authority, of the will to power through merit, spirituality, and self-defense.

If we do not claim and express the power which our High Culture is so desperately urging us to claim and express, we will succumb to the Culture-Pathologies and surely perish before our time.

The question of which Traditions should be preserved and which eliminated, and how the preserved Traditions should be appropriately transformed to serve the new Culture Idea effectively in a new Age with new circumstances is one that can only be answered by the culture-bearing stratum of society who are in tune with the impulses of the High Culture. Recognizing these culture-bearers and mantling them with absolute Authority is the real trick. We must be careful of false messiahs, opportunists, and those who are weak, misguided and impotent. They are nothing more than liars and fools attempting to, at best, enrich themselves, on the average, maintain the status quo of the previous Age, or at worst, destroy our race and civilization. We must learn to recognize the true culture-bearers who are driven by deep instinct and spirit. We must attune ourselves to the spiritual organism of our High Culture and discover through intuition and spiritual self-awareness the Spirit of the Age and act in accordance with it and in support of those who would manifest it in this world.

III

<u>Elite Overproduction and the Modern Crisis</u>

When a culture is in its "civilization" stage, the stage of technics, economic thinking, democracy and rationalism, the main forms of power that act as the mechanism of ascent on the socio-political hierarchy are money and bureaucracy. In other words, in today's world, a person climbs the ladder of success and power by having officially stamped credentials and a large bank account.

One's charisma, spiritual excellence, personality, heroic capabilities, selfless action, talents and other virtuous qualities have little, if anything at all, to do with gaining power and wealth. It is extremely easy for people to gain power in a bureaucratic, money-oriented society. The so-called "playing field" has been leveled. All one needs to do is collect money or pass some academic tests. Anyone at all can do this. There is no excellence required, especially with today's extraordinarily lax academic standards brought on by the scientific materialistic paradigm and democratic beliefs in equality and sameness resulting in the urge toward mediocrity.

This means that the job market for securing elite positions is extremely competitive because there are many millions of people engaged in this rat race. An elite position is an administrative or technical position that is not part of the productive class; essentially any corporate or government office job: i.e: a job that offers as much wealth and power as possible while demanding as little manual labor as possible. It can even include many artistic occupations when an artist wants a money-earning career and easy access to the social ladder choosing to get a degree from an institution and working for the more corporate or governmentally oriented organizations that require the possession of academic degrees as opposed to creating art for more sublime and conscientious reasons which has no guarantee of financial success or social acceptance. These jobs include, but are not limited to, democratically elected politicians, assistants to these politicians, lawyers, business managers, financiers, accountants, pencil pushers and desk jockeys of all sorts, graphic designers, advertising agencies, number crunchers and information sifters, software engineers, hardware engineers, administrators, and so on. Essentially, all the jobs that require an academic degree. Everyone is pressured in their youth, "Go to university, compete for the elite jobs, and secure your freedom and happiness thereby."

And of course, all of these people deny that they are part of the elite or striving to be part of the elite. Holding liberal values, they are endlessly insulted when you tell them that they are in the elite or are elite aspirants by having graduated from university. They believe that the elite are the evil super rich power mongers. They are simply striving to be merely slightly evil moderately rich power mongers. They believe that they are the so-called "educated class" whom I prefer to call the brainwashed elite aspirants. University students and graduates generally love to claim that they are anti-elite, because of course they need to virtue signal that they believe in democratic values, equality, mediocrity, and sameness. Aligning oneself with the dominant mainstream values is part of the modern strategy for effectively securing elite status – something which they will go to great lengths to avoid admitting that they are doing. A "good" person is supposed to be anti-elite. They learned how the world *really* works while attending university. Their Marxist and capitalist professors told them all about it! They know that difference is a sin! They will never admit to wanting to be different, to be "higher" on a social hierarchy that they say should not even exist. Yet, they are climbing it simply as a matter of course, as a given purpose in life, and because they believe that they are the most deserving and qualified to be making political and cultural decisions dictating the future of our culture thanks to the fact they have been enlightened by the university system deeming themselves better than those ignorant working class savages or those vile and arrogant self-taught and alternatively-trained reactionary intellectuals and artists.

These graduates are filling an empty role left open by the destruction of spirituality. At one time, there were excellent people who were truly enlightened by rigorous spiritual training, usually within an initiatic order – a so-called "Mystery School" or an effective spiritual lineage of some kind – or through suffering and deep, difficult life experience that renders them wise, empathic and just. These individuals really were qualified to rule because they underwent a fundamental transformation of consciousness and understood reality and humanity far better than anyone else. Such people possess true wisdom and do not care one iota about being accepted by the masses or being "politically correct." They acted in accordance with Divine Order and instinct, not rationalistic human ignorance. But the rigorous ascetic spiritual training of initiatic orders has been replaced with materialistic education, bureaucratic training and academic hoop-jumping, and those who jump through these academic hoops believe themselves to be the great enlightened initiates of the modern world who deserve to be the ruling elite by virtue of possessing a Holy Diploma from the Church of Accredited Universities or becoming a member of a modern Mystery

School or occult order which are nothing more than fantasy-prone social clubs – mere shells, shams, and perversions of actual occult spiritual orders. (Wearing the regalia of a priest-king and performing the ceremonies of a priest-king does not make one a priest-king. When a monkey wears a suit or a parrot repeats a sentence, they do not become men.)

But again, they will never admit this for fear of appearing hypocritical. *Being* hypocritical is no problem for them. They simply don't want *you* to know that they are hypocrites.

So they attempt to climb, climb, climb the so-called "ladder of success" through economic, bureaucratic, and academic maneuvering. This now defines the entire course of their lives forever, dictated by the distorted culture of materialism, economics, democracy, and rationalism that we are unfortunate enough to be suffering within because "somebody" aborted the 20th century Resurgence of Authority which would have prevented this debacle, this ontological travesty of existence.

***

The elite aspirant problem, in short, is simple. It arises when there are too many elite aspirants and not enough elite jobs. This is called "Elite Overproduction[5]." This means that many people who hoped and dreamed of becoming one of the elite, people who were promised a light at the end of the tunnel, become frustrated by failure to secure an elite position. They dotted every "i", they crossed every "t," they jumped through every hoop, they did everything they were told to do, and yet they failed. These frustrated elite aspirants do not gain the social status, political power or wealth that they were promised and feel a strong sense of resentment, unfairness and injustice. Such people are ripe for deception and can easily become the tools of culture-distorters and culture aliens such as charlatan politicians, social democrats, get-rich-quick financiers, corporate kleptocrats, communist revolutionaries, delusional libertarians, intelligence agencies, malicious cults, fraternities, and terrorist organizations. They want a quick and easy solution for the unwise life choices they were tricked into making after caving in to overwhelming social pressures, economic extortions, and secret criminal conspiracies that lie before us like a minefield that was placed long before we were even born. They desire money and power and they want it now, and they will be easily seduced by any ideology, financial gimmick or political movement that promises it to them.

This is why true revolutions in the positive restorative sense come from above. If revolutions are imagined to come from below, from the masses, (which they in fact never do, they always come from elite social engineers), they come from the dark telluric powers of greed, jealousy, hatred, impotence, frustration and a will to violence, negation, destruction and trickery. Peasant revolts are not the same as revolutions. Only revolutions imbued with the higher spiritual power of Cosmic Order brought into this world by the spiritually excellent aristocratic elite can bring any lasting establishment of justice and creativity in this world – justice that dominates the lower powers of the earth: the chaotic, telluric, chthonic darkness that seduces people to love money, luxury, and ease and to seek hate-filled vengeance against those of whom they are jealous.

The suicidal violence of democratic, communistic revolutions such as those of the French in 1789 and the Bolsheviks in 1917 is offered to frustrated elite aspirants through deception, propaganda, and coercion. This style of revolution is nothing more than trickery foisted upon us by corrupted social engineers and our historical enemies who eternally yearn for vengeance against us and sadistically revel in watching us destroy ourselves.

Such frustrated elite aspirants who have wrought catastrophe and death are scattered throughout the historical record in all High Cultures.

My first example is from Late Medieval France. In the 13th Century, there was a population boom that began two centuries earlier. The population tripled in less than five generations due to the importance and greatness of the French kingdom. It attracted a great deal of immigration. This overwhelmed the capacity of the economy. There were not enough jobs, not enough land to give to peasants, and not enough food for everyone. Most people lived in starvation and poverty during this time, but the wealthy nobles were in a better position to survive through this economic downturn. The noble class (at this time in history determined by money, and only partially by blood, similarly to today) also increased in size faster than the productive class in that landowners and business owners from the peasantry became rich "nobles" due to the high rent prices, high food prices and low wages that they greatly benefitted from. This created a wealth pump from the productive class to the wealthy class – the rich got richer as the poor got poorer[5].

As their income increased, "noble" families became more savvy in securing their wealth – dividing their extra land and business assets and money amongst all of their sons instead of just giving it all to the oldest, each of their children was now able to become a middle rank or low rank elite and the numbers of elite having sufficient income to remain in the "nobility" skyrocketed. The social pyramid became very top-heavy.

But now, there was less and less cheap plentiful labor seeing that many peasants were becoming elite. These elite could not maintain their income as wages had to competitively increase as the workforce shrank, so they sought employment from the state demanding higher taxes from the productive class off of which they could live. But of course, there are not that many government jobs available in a given society and increased taxes caused inflation and the royal treasury was being depleted by these elites demanding income.

The higher taxes also caused landlords to begin stealing from their tenants and generally oppressing them for more wealth extraction.

All of these economic programs exacerbated the problems and the elites began fighting and competing amongst themselves.

In 1328, the king died without leaving a male heir and three claimants for the throne warred against each other which caused instability and set the conditions for peasant rebellions to simultaneously occur. There was complete state collapse of the French Kingdom by 1360.

Then, the following generation of elites, not having lived through this terrible time, repeated the mistakes of their parents and continued extracting wealth from the peasants and fighting amongst themselves. By 1415, there was another total collapse – they were conquered by the British while peasant rebellions, famines and epidemics plagued the kingdom.

By 1453, the French reconquered their kingdom and the problem seemed to be solved by this terrible century of war, poverty, starvation, and disease which reduced the total population by about 60% which included a reduction of the elite by 75% who died in battle or in intra-elite massacres. The social pyramid was no longer very top-heavy. There was finally enough land, cheap rent, and higher wages for the peasantry to live higher quality lives. The memory of the British occupation gave the elite a united national cause and feeling against a shared enemy and they implemented economic reforms which were favorable for everyone in the kingdom for generations to come.

We can see that the solutions for Elite Overproduction and popular suffering in this case were massive waves of death and war with an outsider. Not very pleasant or sustainable solutions in my opinion. These solutions were forced upon the French people by nature and social law. Nature and social law only overtake cultures who lack self-awareness, who have no sense of history, who have no will to acknowledge their problems, and are blinded by greed. If a culture cannot muster the spiritual excellence to solve these problems politically, nature will provide solutions in the form of depopulation, destructive war with outsiders, and destructive intra-cultural massacres – in other words: revolution from below.

As I said earlier, the lower forces of the earth are destructive and chaotic – they are the forces of negation. They are the chthonic and telluric forces that do not give a damn about human beings or their welfare. These forces are not creative or orderly or positive in any way. If a culture fails to rally their inner forces of creativity, order, and positive political action, they will automatically suffer the forces of negation and destruction in the natural course of time.

My next historical example is from the Qing Dynasty Era of China (1644-1912). That society was ruled by bureaucratic scholar-administrators similar to the modern West. Elite aspirants had to pass some exams dealing with Confucian political science. The more exams they passed, the higher up the ranks they moved; again, very similar to our university degree system which goes from a high school diploma to a two-year college degree to a bachelors degree to a masters degree to a doctorate and includes any number of certifications in between these ranks.

In the Qing dynasty, this helped with literacy among the elite and provided a shared sense of culture and morality via the Confucian Classics. Unfortunately, our modern Western education system does not have this internal cultural benefit as our system is controlled by culture-distorters. But even a relatively good, functional system like the Qing is still vulnerable to population growth. The administrative industry simply does not grow with the population. More and more people attended these schools and took these exams so more and more people felt entitled to elite jobs. One ineffectual solution was to make the higher rank exams artificially more difficult to score well. Our modern situation is just as bad in terms of population growth and even worse in terms of cultural distortion and disunion caused by an education system infected by foreign, outmoded, outdated and destructive ideologies.

By 1850, there was an enormous population of frustrated elite aspirants with no hopes of getting the job they wanted and an entire population of impoverished, starving people resulting from essentially the same conditions as in our French example. Enter Hong Xiuquan – a frustrated elite aspirant; a third son from a rich family who went to the best schools and had the best tutors money could buy. He achieved what would today be called a masters degree, but failed to achieve the imperial (or doctorate) degree. This led to a period of depression and illness. During this time, his mind was polluted by the culture-parasites and culture-distorters from the West who had entered China at this time in the form of Christian missionaries and businessmen. In this period, Westerners were to China what the Jewish are to the West. He was taken in by the leveling egalitarianism and anti-hierarchical values of Christianity and democracy. He created a new religious cult called the Society of God Worshipers based on these democratic Christian values which was very attractive to the poor suffering masses. The Chinese authorities attempted to suppress his movement, and this triggered the Taiping Rebellion which some historians consider to be bloodiest revolution in recorded history.

Other rebellions of a similar nature led by frustrated elite aspirants with similar stories erupted all over China at this same time. Not to mention, similar revolutions were occurring in Europe as well. However, in 1864, Hong died and these rebellions were suppressed by the military leader Zeng Guofan and the Qing dynasty survived this conflagration until of course the world revolution of World War One broke out and liberalism began to galvanize its place as the new world order.

And needless to say, Vladimir Ulyonov (a.k.a. Lenin) and Lev Bronstein (a.k.a. Leon Trotsky) were also wealthy frustrated elite aspirants and members of the cultural-alien diaspora in Russia. They acted as culture-distorters taking advantage of the same conditions that led to popular immiseration, poverty and suffering caused by industrialization, overpopulation, and overproduction of elites. But in this case, the ruling elite actually had decent historical sense and self-awareness, including the Tsar's Prime Minister and Minister of the Interior Pyotr Stolyapin. He attempted to reform the economy to benefit everyone, slowly turning serfs into land-owning peasants and suppressing communist revolutionaries. However, his life and program were cut short by a Jewish assassin and his policies were canceled after the Tsar abdicated and of course he and the entire Royal Family were executed by more Jewish assassins. Stolyapin was performing his duties properly by exercising authority and making sure the economy functioned for everyone, benefitting all while maintaining the hierarchical structure of his culture. But of course, rationalistic revolutionaries do not want to solve problems with creativity, hierarchy, honor or nobility. They want to exacerbate problems so they can have orgies of blood and destruction which allows them to climb the ladder of chaos and become the masters of money and the new political elite while exacting vengeance upon their historical enemies.

What Stolyapin attempted was called "compression" according to Peter Turchin[5]. When there is popular suffering and elite overproduction, history generally offers two solutions: revolution, death and destruction, or compression. Basically, these options can be seen as revolution from below or revolution from above. Compression is revolution from above. The elite see the problem, feel a sense of responsibility and cultural unity, and decide to solve the problem by mobilizing resources and giving up their hoarded wealth and reconfiguring the laws and the economy to benefit everyone.

This actually occurred in the United States just after World War Two when the number of millionaires in the country dropped significantly from about 50 to about 15 when they all decided to re-invest into the nation. Real wages skyrocketed, inflation decreased, property became affordable, and the middle class seemed to be a solid reality taken for granted. This occurred because the wealthy elite felt a sense of responsibility and cultural cohesion and wanted to avoid a terrible revolution and disintegration of their society.

It is a tragic problem with our historical propaganda apparatus in our schooling system that our historians fail to acknowledge the fact that the United States was one bad day away from a terrible bloody revolution in the late 1940's. The Great Depression destroyed countless lives and stole wealth from nearly everyone and gave it to the culture-distorters. Not to mention, the nation had just fought a war that no one wanted to be part of; they were coerced into killing their European brothers and sisters for absolutely no reason but to pretend that they were protecting democracy and the cultural-alien that they were supposed to have greater compassion for than for their own people. To avoid this revolution, the policy of compression was implemented. However, it lasted only about one generation before our problems began to return because they were not solved at a fundamental spiritual level, they merely put economic band-aids on this spiritual gunshot wound to pacify the population, to buy themselves some time, so to speak.

Well, the time they bought is very nearly up.

The same age-old choices lie before us: ignore the problem and allow bloody revolutions and natural disasters to sweep the land, or replace the economic elite with a spiritual elite.

We need to dig deep within ourselves and initiate ourselves spiritually through self-awareness and self-control training. We must fundamentally transform our consciousness and stop loving money. We must destroy the power of money and the enticing hold it has over our souls. This will make us immune to communist propaganda and capitalist/libertarian greed-based solutions rooted in degenerate economic thinking. This will render us impervious to the poisonous and self-destructive ideas offered to us by the culture-distorters. We must suppress the entirely negative influence of the culture-distorters and discover within ourselves solutions to these problems; solutions which are rooted in Cosmic Hierarchy and create a complete positive system of values to replace the outdated, outmoded, negative and destructive values of the 18th and 19th centuries – ideologies which have outlived their welcome and are kept artificially in power by the culture-distorters. We must create these new values and rediscover the old ones that are distinctly and instinctively ours – from our own innermost subjective reality. And through the application of our own spiritually-anointed authority, we will sweep away the degeneracy and corruption that has taken hold of our culture.

To hell with elite overproduction. Render bureaucracy and money irrelevant by becoming spiritually excellent, spiritually superior to all those who consider themselves today's elite. If they want money, you must want honor. If they seek credentials, you must seek the spiritual chrism. If they want arbitrary obedience, you must be able to inspire natural obedience, action and loyalty. Undermine them through your spiritual excellence. Be better than them in every way.

IV

<u>True Hierarchy and How to Create It</u>

Most people in today's world consider hierarchy to be some bureaucratic framework and infrastructure that exists with offices and positions which are then filled by candidates who have passed some test or graduated from some institution or have succeeded in some type of popularity contest. While this is indeed a form of hierarchy, it is entirely artificial, unreal, contrived, unnatural and the offices and positions will be filled by unworthy people. This sort of hierarchy can efficiently work for one or two generations before cheating, nepotism, simony and all forms of skullduggery conquer its mecahnisms.

Let us reexamine the elite aspirant problem through the lens of hierarchy.

When a culture is in the stage of rationalism, economic thinking, technical thinking and democracy (also known as its "civilization" stage), an ideology of egalitarianism, sameness and enforced mediocrity sets in. Excellence and difference are frowned upon and natural hierarchy is questioned and no longer trusted. Kings are beheaded and revolutionary "democracies" operating on capitalistic and communistic

53

economies are established. Hierarchy is then determined by money and ascended by a bureaucratic rat race. Winning the rat race is achieved by a candidate checking boxes on a spreadsheet. Employers and governments look to see who will be their most competent slaves according to their machine-like, inhuman labor expectations. The employee or "public servant" is not seen as a unique soulful human person but as a machine to do a job, and that job is to increase the monetary gains of the company for the owners or to piddle about in the bureaucratic corridors of the government securing the illusory power held by politicians insuring that they are able to enrich themselves while pretending to serve society.

The highest paying jobs that everyone wants – the so-called "elite" jobs – are corporate office jobs and government office jobs. Of course in a "democracy," people seek to do the least amount of work for the most amount of money. People become qualified for these jobs by attending and graduating from a brainwashing camp… pardon me… a university. Upon being thoroughly indoctrinated and passing some tests, proof of indoctrination is given in the form of a diploma or a certificate, the highest form of indoctrination of course being the aptly named doctorate. Now a person is entitled to an elite job. Or so they are told.

A fundamental characteristic of corporate and government industries, the inappropriately named "service industry," or what I prefer to call the financial - bureaucratic - administrative industry, is that it barely grows no matter how much the population grows. A given society does not need that many number crunchers, government clerks, financiers, politicians, software or hardware engineers, information sifters, administrators or managers. These industries cap out at a relatively small critical mass and no more people are required for this industry to function properly.

But these are the highest paying jobs with the most political authority and social status and the least amount of actual labor. Everyone is told to go to university and compete for these jobs, because that is the key to money and money is equated with happiness, power and freedom according to our modern degenerate values. So, more and more people every year are filling this competitive job market which has basically the same number of jobs that it has always had and will always have. Sure, we sometimes artificially inflate the number of jobs available by inventing useless fake jobs like human resources and intra-office facilitation or by increasing the number of useless managers and administrators in a given workspace. But these are ineffective solutions that everyone hates and resents because of how obviously wasteful, insipid and stupid they are.

Peter Turchin describes this very well. Imagine playing a game of musical chairs, but instead of removing a chair every time the music stops, the number of chairs remains the same and each round, ten new players are added to the game[5]. It will not be long before people begin cheating, standing in front of an empty chair and blocking everyone from approaching it while the music is playing so they may claim it, saving chairs for their friends and family, paying off the DJ to stop the song at a particular time, setting up booby traps to break the ankles of unsuspecting players, bribing the referee to look the other way when they pull out a knife and shank their competitors. You get the idea. Welcome to the modern world. This is what a modern hierarchy is – the end result of money-thinking and democracy. People ascend this hierarchy through worthless bureaucratic credentials, wearing a false persona, nepotism, finance, lying, flattery, deal-making, self-debasement, backstabbing, distrust, and crime. Basically, you need to betray your own cultural heritage and ethics in one way or another to ascend this hierarchy. Virtually no one ascends this hierarchy through honor and nobility as those who possess such qualities are ridiculed, laughed at and seen as "problematic" anachronisms by those who hold liberal values.

The solution is not some economic program or a change in policy – although, those will inevitably come downstream from the real solution. The real solution is far deeper than that. This is a spiritual problem and requires a spiritual transformation.

In a "democracy," people despise excellence and difference. There is a great will to level everyone and everything to mediocrity and sameness. Arguably, in Western civilization, this stems from Christianity, this belief that anyone who strives for spiritual excellence is corrupted by Luciferian arrogance or self-worship. This dual disease of Christianity and democracy in the Western world has eliminated the natural, organic hierarchy that all normal, healthy, traditional civilizations have. It has deceived everyone into humbling (a.k.a humiliating) themselves even though they may be able to achieve greatness. It has deceived everyone into hating and being jealous of all those people who are better than themselves, who excel in some field, who have more charisma, more self-awareness, more self-control, more dignity, more honor, more talent, a greater sense of duty, justice and righteousness, and a more advanced spirituality – especially if these qualities were achieved outside of the university system or outside of Christian institutions. The people who are deeply lost and confused and infected and brainwashed by culture distortions sneer at these great individuals and gossip about them calling them arrogant, self-righteous, demon-possessed, Luciferian, problematic, retrogressive, false-prophets, reactionary and so on. But people with a healthy attitude skeptical of liberal, rationalistic values from the Enlightenment Era and Christian weaknesses and dogma, people who have at least some self-awareness and self-control are inspired by these excellent people, follow their example, serve them and their vision and manifest it into this world thereby improving and fulfilling the culture, and then they seek within themselves the attitude and discipline necessary to cultivate so that they too may achieve such greatness.

Simply put, excellent people inspire and uplift others. They bring order to the world around themselves. Action occurs around them without them acting at all due to their imperious commanding presence. This is what the Eastern traditions and occult Western traditions mean when they say, "Acting without acting, the sage accomplishes all things[6]." They are different from those around themselves and it is obvious to everyone. People want to follow and be led by such individuals. A hierarchy will naturally form underneath them without any preexisting bureaucratic framework in place; without any official policy or political infrastructure that needs to be filled by candidates.

People who are near them in spiritual quality but not quite equal will happily be their subordinates. And the people who are near these ones but not quite equal will subordinate themselves and so on. This is a living fact I can attest to from my own experience. Look for it in the historical record and in the world around you; in your own life, and you will see it, too.

When you are around someone who is truly spiritually excellent, you will know it. When you meet someone who is worthy of your admiration and loyalty, there is no mistaking it, so long as you are mentally and spiritually healthy and hygienic yourself – not suffering from things like jealousy, envy, greed, hatred, susceptibility to propaganda and others' ideas, and so on. If you are poisoned by the beliefs in liberalism, democracy, economic thinking, capitalism, communism and other 19th century ideas and their concomitant spiritual diseases like hedonism, jealousy, delusion, and the lack of self-awareness and self-control, you can easily be misled by people who appear excellent on the surface, such as flatterers, charlatans, rhetoricians, charismatic opportunists, and predators as can easily be seen by the electoral processes of modern politics and the cult-like activity permeating the social, religious and spiritual spheres.

This is why liberals, believers in democracy, rationalists, capitalists and communists are untrusting of leaders and great people, why they hate them and encourage others to hate them as well, because they themselves are easily deceived into following terrible people and lack the capacity to discern a great spiritual leader from a simple arrogant ass. They don't know what greatness looks like because individual greatness belongs to the realms of Honor, Chivalry and Spiritual Difference; three things which the modern world have turned their backs on and destroyed in the name of their degenerate values and vices called progress, equality, and the pursuit of happiness. Only in an imperial or clan-based society can Honor, Chivalry and Spiritual Difference flourish. In a democratic society, these things are labeled as dangerous, misogynistic, outdated, laughable, superstitious, retrogressive and racially supremacist. But these virtues are easily recognized by people who have even a small amount of spiritual discipline or disposition within themselves.

But we all know, either consciously or instinctively, that a society must have a hierarchy to function. Without hierarchy, there is anarchy, and no culture or civilization is possible under anarchic conditions. Democracy and Christianity are urges toward anarchy; they are inherently anti-civilization: Christianity (with its world-denial and its hatred of powerful cultures, believing that all worldly power is ultimately satanic) and liberalism (with its desire to atomize everyone and level everything) make Higher Cultural activity impossible. So what did we do to protect our dogmatic beliefs in liberalism and Christianity and reconcile those leveling urges toward equality and mediocrity while maintaining a functioning society? We invented the bureaucratic hierarchy which we are all currently lamenting and suffering from. Everyone has an equal opportunity to climb the bureaucratic hierarchy by gaining certification from some institution or collecting money. Any and all need for charisma, honor, chivalry, spiritual excellence, duty, responsibility, and difference are legally stripped away and any fool with a degree or a large wallet is qualified to make political, economic, artistic, and cultural decisions for society. This bureaucratic hierarchy is seen as a happy medium between natural authority and complete anarchy. Natural authority, the enemy of Christians and liberals, is stifled to the point of elimination and has no place to flourish or express itself (except for perhaps in the ranks of the military on foreign battlefields), and people can feel a bit anarchic and equal with the notion that anyone at all can climb the bureaucratic hierarchy, and they can satisfy their instinctual need for hierarchy by climbing this type of social ladder.

Difference is clearly still desired as can be seen by the generally abhorrent just-below-the-surface arrogance of university graduates who think they are wiser, more moral and more deserving of power than everyone else simply because they got brainwashed by mainstream ideology and have the paperwork to prove it.

This desire for difference flies in the face of their liberal values and belief in equality rendering these types hypocrites with multiple personality disorder, saying one thing when it is socially and politically convenient, but doing another thing because they desire to have power over others and have arrogated that power to themselves through bureaucratic maneuvering, academic test taking, and wealth acquisition. They are utterly unable to inspire confidence and loyalty in people due to their complete lack of spirituality, dignity, talent, self-awareness, and self-control, yet they believe they deserve respect and obedience because they have a piece of paper that says they are entitled to it, or simply because they make more money than someone else. They believe certifications and money are divine investitures signifying their worth and authority. This is the worldview of Calvinism (the logical conclusion of Christianity) and the ideas of Karl Marx and Adam Smith, the main ideologues of communism and capitalism; liberals par excellence.

Such a hierarchy is fundamentally flawed and cannot be corrected because the framework for the hierarchy itself is born of the cultural diseases and pathologies that infect our society.

The solution is to create a new elite. We must render the current elite powerless and irrelevant by becoming spiritually excellent ourselves and replacing them through sheer force of will and charisma; by our very presence and existence. This will and charisma comes from adherence to the great spiritual Tradition, through self-awareness training which leads to self-control, which leads to true initiation – a radical and immense transformation of consciousness that renders one as different from other people as a human is different from the animals. A gulf of difference is created between a spiritually elite person and everyone else. Look at the sages, magicians, prophets, adepts and great men throughout history from all cultures. The possibility of being one of these great men is your birthright if you have the fortitude, endurance, will, perseverance, self-possession, vitality, and singularness of focus to walk such a lonely, arduous and estranging path. But it is the highest path. It is the most difficult thing a person can do and you must sacrifice all that you have and wish for in order to succeed.

This new elite will be recognized as superior to the old elite simply by observation and comparison.

Why is it that at the age of eighteen, I could stand on stage at a forum in front of two thousand people in a university auditorium next to doctors of economics, political science, and philosophy giving talks on the problems of the day, saying things in utter contradistinction from these so-called experts, and the crowd during the

Q and A session would consult with only me, ignoring the others with whom I shared the stage? Their ideas and personalities were considered utterly uninteresting compared with mine even though they had decades of academic experience behind them.

Why is it that at the Occupy Wall Street movement in Manhattan, I could stand on a bench with a megaphone and with a few short sentences, earn the ire, jealousy and hatred of the communists, liberals and bankers who were there, while gaining the unquestioning loyalty of the crowd and the sympathy of the police force while providing them an adequate and satisfying criticism of modernity that inspired them to search for their own solutions? (And did you ever see me on the news in those days? I was interviewed by about a dozen journalists and filmed by three documentarians but was entirely stricken from the record.)

Why is it that with every collaborative artistic endeavor I enter into, even with total strangers, immediately everyone on the team refers to me to determine the foundation and direction of the creative possibilities and asks me to lead the delegation of work and judge the final result, even though I do not insist on leading anything or anyone?

Why is it that wherever I go, I am immediately treated like a trusted psychotherapist and confidant, a spiritual counselor, a priest, and wise teacher by friends, family and strangers alike without anyone doubting or questioning this anointment?

Why is it that whenever I enter a room full of people, suddenly the mood changes to whatever my current mood is and I dictate the emotional ebbs and flows for the entire time I am present without doing anything at all?

Forgive me for the self-indulgence, but this is a real life example of what I am talking about. I speak from my own experience. I know what I'm saying is true. I am not simply regurgitating the words of the stoics, Taoists, Hindus, or the modern occultists. I am a living example of this invisible authority that is automatically recognized by others. I have no academic degree. I have no money. I have no social, political or economic status to speak of. This command of the external world is the result of true spiritual discipline; of real spiritual power. I do not need to flaunt my money, or frame a diploma and hang it on the wall, or show my business card, or relay my past exploits on a resume. I simply enter a place, and people feel the air change, the energy shift, and I am automatically recognized and respected by sane, healthy people. Obviously, I am hated by the enemies of spirituality, regality and difference. They also recognize me immediately without knowing anything about me. It is a subtle force that emanates from a person that others are influenced by and can feel.

Most people love to be around such individuals. We refresh and enliven others, fill them with spiritual energy and interesting new ideas, discharge their nervous systems and lighten their mood and alleviate stress. We bring out the best in others and encourage everyone to be who they truly are. We listen to your troubles and help put you at ease and open a new chapter in your life. We also have an unwavering sense of justice and make terrifying enemies with indomitable wills, so we also fill people with a sense of comfort, protection and inspiration by standing for what is right against the forces of evil, degeneration, darkness, and chaos in any situation and we are not afraid to take that stance immediately and swiftly and be stern about it even if it costs us our popularity.

A friend of mine once told me that I was born either a thousand years too late or a thousand years too soon; my words and actions seem to come from another time or another world entirely, and this inspires, frightens and perplexes people.

In the courtroom, our word becomes more influential and just than the word of the Judges. In the classroom, our wisdom becomes more helpful than the science and citations of the professor. In the senate chambers, our common sense becomes more authoritative and sensible than the written law. In the social sphere, our generosity, loyalty and high standards become the foundations for tribes, communities and local governments. In the military, our dignity, courage and forthrightness become the morale and might of the warriors in our ranks. In the economic sphere, our fairness and sense of stewardship become the seeds of prosperity and shines a light on the greed of the parasites.

All this is simply because we are fundamentally, internally different from most people. We do not cave in to their pressures, their enticements, their bribes, their desires, their dogmas, their beliefs, their mediocre mentality, or their mental illnesses and corruption. We search within ourselves for our own subjective reality and live by it. We do what we will to do as individuals, resistant to propaganda and social pressures, and it inspires the hell out of everyone around us to the shock, horror and resentment of those whose authority rests merely on credentials, money and bureaucracy.

Our authority rests in spirit and shines forth in charisma, an unquantifiable, irrational power that the bureaucrats, rationalists and money-thinkers cannot comprehend, buy, sell, or compete against. We are irresistible. Everything around us finds order and falls neatly into its natural place and people feel free and more productive and more lively when we are around. The current corrupt unnatural elite cannot stand this about us. This is why we are so reviled and ridiculed and persecuted in the mainstream and in the snobby social circles. It is why we are excluded and exiled.

These bureaucratic and economic elite must be replaced by spiritually excellent people if we are to know real freedom, prosperity and cultural restoration. It won't be easy, nor will it happen quickly, but real meaningful revolutions are seeds planted and nourished, not short-lived conflagrations and orgies of bloodshed. If we want to develop a real culture with real roots that vitalize future generations, this is how it will be accomplished.

To begin this journey of true spiritual awakening, one must practice self-awareness training, self-control, and bring about real initiation, which is a fundamental transformation of consciousness. We can begin with some books, although ultimately you will depend only on yourself and not on books or on other people's ideas when you realize that you are utterly sufficient unto yourself and lack nothing:

- *Meditations* by Marcus Aurelius
- *The Tao te Ching* by Lao Tzu
- *The Bhagavad Gita*
- *The Ramayana*
- *The Yoga Sutras* by Patanjali
- *The Shiva Samhita*
- *In Search of the Miraculous* by P.D. Ouspensky

- *How to Know Higher Worlds* by Rudolf Steiner
- *Introduction to Magic Vol. I – III* by Julias Evola and the Ur Group
- *Pagan Imperialism* by Julius Evola
- *Initiation into Hermetics* by Franz Bardon

These books will help awaken within you the ability to know yourself, to look at yourself with complete and total honesty, and to overcome the darkness and chaos of your lower nature without pacifying you or eliminating the power that can be derived from within you.

Who is better? The one who has conquered a city or the one who has conquered himself? One is king for a day, the other, king for eternity.

V

<u>The Oak and the Grass</u>

So who exactly are the counter-elite who are destined to replace the current elite? Generally speaking, they are the ones who are simultaneously well-liked and reviled, praised and ridiculed, celebrated and looked down upon. Have you ever heard a person say about someone else, "He is so smart and interesting, why doesn't he succeed in life?" or "If he only applied himself and stopped dreaming, he could achieve so much!" or "He is a late-bloomer" or "He is a jack of all trades, master of none" even though he has mastered at least a few or "He is an uncommitted dabbler who abandons everything he begins and moves on to new interests which he will eventually abandon" or some other such thing that attacks the financially unsuccessful polymath and laments that he has refused the path of specialization and money-orientation that everyone else takes?

Such people spend roughly the first half of their life analyzing reality and suffering in ways most others cannot even begin to comprehend even when it is explained to them. While most people are climbing their ladders to "success," this person is examining the wall that the ladders are leaned against and thinks to himself, "This wall is terrible. This is the wrong wall to lean your ladder against." Everyone replies, "But this is the only wall! This is the wall we all must climb, you fool!"

And so this person takes their ladder down and looks for a new wall to lean it against or perhaps he must first find new mortar and stone to build himself a wall worthy of his dignity.

While most people are learning the rules of the game and trying to win, this person asks, "Why is this game even being played at all? Who invented this game? Who wrote its rules?" Everyone replies, "Are you insane? There is no game! This is how life works! You will fail if you think like that!"

And so this person stops playing the game to the confusion and resentment of everyone else.

He is told that his interests are too many, that he must commit to a specialization and do nothing but that in order to earn money, otherwise he will be left behind. But his interests are not too many. He is learning all he wants and needs. They are not random interests and activities, they are a constellation of stars he is building within his soul; they are ingredients of a recipe that no one has ever cooked before. He is diving into the depths of life and reality, analyzing and experiencing all he can to find the treasures of meaning contained within these seemingly disparate hobbies and endeavors. Throughout his early life, while his soul urges him to these new interests and to abandon the old ones when their meaning and depth have been exhausted for him, he knows not why, not yet, but one day, it will coalesce and come together, usually when he is in his late thirties or early forties.

Everyone else picked a specialization and stuck to it. They achieved their financial security in their twenties. They got their spouse, their white picket fence, their 2.2 cars and 1.8 children. They "won" the game of life. But what these people do not have is emotional intelligence, spiritual depth, psychological knowledge, well-developed intuition, empathy, historical sense, a sense of justice, an understanding of deeper meanings, an appreciation for the mysteries of reality and the expansive nature of consciousness, a holistic view of reality, pattern recognition, predicting capabilities, the ability to endure long suffering. They have forgone developing any depth in their lives in exchange for money, sex, luxury and property. They look at the polymath and think, "What a failure. He hasn't even begun to climb the ladder we climbed! He is so lost! He has achieved nothing!"

And unfortunately, the polymath also feels this about themselves to varying degrees depending on their self-awareness and societal-awareness. They may wonder why they can't hold a job or an interest for very long. They may lament that they do not possess the money and sex and property that everyone else has and can't seem to get it because it has no real appeal or meaning to them, or in order to get it, they must sacrifice their dignity and the calling of their soul which they are naturally disinclined to do.

Nobody gets paid for increasing their spiritual knowledge. No one earns a salary for gaining wisdom. Nobody is rewarded for learning to control their emotions. No one receives a paycheck for knowing their self. Nobody gets a seat in the government for understanding how consciousness works. The greatest inner achievements in life are unrecognized and unrewarded by society.

The so-called "late bloomer" suffers immeasurably in the first half of his life. He sees the world as it is from a very young age. Skipping his childhood and entering adulthood at the age of five, having been born with a penetrating insight, he feels keenly the ontological nightmare that is human existence. He has plumbed the darkest depths of reality and self and has seen into the void of cosmic horror. He has dwelt as an outsider, an exile in his own home, misunderstood by almost everyone he has ever met. He does not desire what most people desire. He does not pursue the type of fleeting ephemeral happiness that most people believe is the very goal of life. He has seen through the deceptions and illusions to which everyone is fully subject and he weeps for their slavish ignorance to these phantasms. An awakened man in a kingdom of sleepers, he is resented for his awareness. A truth-perceiving man, he lives as a subject in a kingdom ruled by liars and scoundrels who wish for nothing less than his undoing simply because he sees them and knows their tricks. Living in a world that applauds the youthful prodigy and the early successes who speed down the straight road, he is made to feel like a failure for taking a winding, slow and contemplative road. An honorable man in a society motivated by dishonor, he is laughed at for his chivalry, exploited for his kindness, trampled over for his empathy, spurned for his loving heart, resented for his standards, ridiculed for his incorruptible code of conduct, mistrusted because he does not commit crime, alone because he does not debauch himself, he feels utterly lost, abandoned by God in a world that does not suit him.

Most people never experience this type of suffering. They cannot comprehend it or imagine it. But it is this very suffering and pain that develops empathy, wisdom, justice, righteousness, incorruptibility, fortitude, endurance through hardship, spiritual awareness, intuition, the willingness to help and console others who suffer, the ability to transform the perceptions and perspectives of others, and infinitely more virtues and powers besides.

These very virtues and more are what make such a one worthy of holding and wielding immense power on the political, cultural, and spiritual levels. Normal people seem to be corrupted by power, but it is because they were already corrupt themselves. Power merely amplifies who a person already is. Lord Acton and William Pitt were utterly mistaken when they made the claim that power corrupts. A long-suffering, virtuous, empathic and wise person can wield absolute power with great benefit to the people at large. They, in fact, are the only people in existence worthy of possessing power.

So I have a word of wisdom for the so-called "late bloomer" who is in fact a member of the coming elite: the oak does not grow at the same pace as the grass. The grass will be fully formed and matured in a single season. The oak takes many seasons. The blade of grass will whither and die in short order and be replaced by new blades rapidly, killed by the first drop in temperature. The oak will endure many winters, singular and mighty. The grass produces very little of worth aside from erosion control. Birds will nest and raise their young in the branches of the oak. People will take shelter and have enjoyments under its canopy. Wizard staffs and magic wands are fashioned from its boughs. Great structures will be built with its wood. And eventually, the oak produces acorns which become new mighty oaks.

A small pair of scissors can threaten the blade of grass. A single inclement cold snap or drought will bring an entire field of grass to ruin. It takes a strong and persistent lumberjack or a hurricane of immense magnitude to fell an oak. The first emotional crisis can ruin the lives of an immature married couple. The loss of money or a specialized job can result in an irreparable psychological shock that can undo a person who has no spiritual wisdom. Political ebbs and flows will drive superficial people mad with rage and elation. The midlife crisis will hit people who achieved their successes in their twenties and thirties once they gain a little depth and wisdom later in life. This inkling of wisdom that comes with age will have them come crashing headlong into the meaninglessness of money, the banalities of their spouses' personality, the tidal disturbances of political imbalances, the vapidness of the choices they made, the weaknesses of the foundation they built, the incorrectness of the ideologies they believed, and the yawning maw between their ignorant mind and the knowledge of reality. Such a midlife crisis hits most people and the rest of their lives are spent trying to gratify themselves with more meaningless enjoyments or struggling to find meaning – the meaning that the "late bloomer" found by age twelve. Those who sprint through the early part of their lives are generally shallow, unwise and unprepared for trials and hardships.

The difference between a "successful" 40 year old man and a 40 year old "late bloomer" is that the late bloomer's worst years are behind him. The successful man's worst years are in front of him.

To those who are younger but feel their inherent "late bloomer" characteristics, take heart and endure. Follow the urgings of your soul and care not for the opinions of others. When you have achieved the true age of maturity, the true beginning of adulthood between 35 and 45, you will see your life transform for the better, but you must act in the world at that age to see it done. As long as you are learning, growing, and disciplining yourself in the meantime, do not worry about lack of worldly achievement before the age of maturity.

To all of my "late bloomer" readers, around age 35 to 45, you must begin your great work. Stop pretending that you need to learn more or analyze more or wait for the right time. You are far wiser and more intelligent than the people who currently write your laws, regulate your economy, create works of art, and preserve and promulgate scientific and spiritual knowledge. You are far worthier than they of possessing power, teaching wisdom and publishing works. Do not let your desire to be kind, modest and unassuming blind you to this fact. Do not worry about how the game is normally played; do not worry about how the players will receive you. Kick the table over and scatter the pieces to the floor. It is not arrogance; your superiority is a simple anthropological fact. At this age in your life, humility is humiliation. You must start creating and doing something now and plow over or remove the people from your life who would get in your way. If you are to become the counter-elite, now is the time to act.

Take all those parts of you that you suppressed in your youth: your anger, your ambition, your assertiveness, your disgust for modernity, your disdain for the corrupt, and unleash them upon the world. You suppressed them because you wanted to be a good person. You had empathy for those who deserved your anger. You had compassion for those who do wrong. While this does you credit and trained your soul for goodness and wisdom, now your empathy and compassion is to be reserved only for the people who deserve it. Allow everyone else to recoil at the searing heat of your fiery boundaries – the flaming border of your life that only a select few may cross. And whether close or kept at a distance, everyone will have changed in some way simply for having known you.

The world needs to be reminded of what Honor, Courage, Wisdom and Duty really mean. They must know that the Order of Cosmic Law is absolute and shall be upheld before the chaos of man's law. If you are the Instrument of God's Wrath, be that instrument now. If you are the Voice of God's Indignation, speak with that voice now. If you are the Love of God's Heart, love with that heart now. If you are the Cudgel in the Judge's hand or the Sword in the Holy Scabbard, do what you were forged to do.

You can rest when you are dead.

Your best years are ahead of you.

VI

<u>Race is Spiritual</u>

"Materialism is shallow, especially when applied to living things. The spirit is primary and matter is simply the vehicle for the expression of the spirit."[7]

"Race is not group anatomy. Race is not independent of the soil. Race is not independent of spirit and history. Races are not classifiable except on an arbitrary basis. Race is not a rigid permanent collective characterization of human beings, which remains the same always throughout history... Race [is] fluid, gliding with history over the fixed skeletal form determined by the soil."[4]

Before you accuse me of some form of neo-Marxist spiritualism, understand that these were a paraphrase from Oswald Spengler, the great 20th Century philosopher of civilization who is often quoted by the modern Right, and a quote from Francis Yockey, a man so far to the right, he made Mussolini look like a girl scout. These quotes simply show a total rejection of materialism and the outmoded sciences that were born from it. They show a complete conviction in spirituality.

Carl Jung, when visiting America for the first time, saw a group of miners, all white men, and believed that they were the product of thorough blood mixing with American Indians[8]. They had all the body type features of the American Indian save the colors of their skin, hair and eyes. He assumed they all must have had some American Indian parents or grandparents. When he expressed this to his American guide, it was made quite clear to him that each man there had not a single drop of Indian blood, but was purely and entirely white as far back as their families can be remembered.

I'm going to commit the cardinal sin of referencing Franz Boas, a Jewish anthropologist, pro-communist, and globalist. He made accurate observations about the physical features of people from all over the world while taking careful note of their genealogy. He discovered that the children of immigrants immediately, with the very first generation, take on the skeletal features and body types of the people who commonly live in their new environment[9]. Now of course he used this research to show that there is no such thing as race, there is only the human race, and this is a strong talking point for the globalists, capitalists, and communists, seeing as they are anti-spiritual and utterly materialistic in their outlook. But his observations on the physical biological features of people are truthful and accurate. The data is there and it is irrefutable. Simply look around you; you can usually tell when someone is an American and not a German or an Englishman or an African or an Asian just by seeing a photo of them. All of our skeletons have changed, and they belong to a particular type of geospatial aesthetic.

Further research of this type has been carried out by people such as Clarence Gravlee[10]. Setting aside their tangential, lopsided and unfortunate political interpretations of their own data and observations, take a look at their data for yourself and come to your own conclusions and interpretations.

It is also interesting to note that indigenous people from all over the world generally have a common belief that you cannot conquer a land and move your people there, because they will inherit the ancestral spirits of that land and become their people.

Rupert Sheldrake has his theory of morphic resonance[11], which is based on Goethe's theory of urpflanze[12]. Basically, organic materials and living entities like minerals, plants, animals, and people produce an energetic field around themselves which affects and influences other materials and organisms within its range, oftentimes altering the physical shape and characteristics. Rudolf Steiner, the 20th Century mystic and clairvoyant, noted that geomagnetic forces created by the minerals of a place effect the skeletal structure of people[13].

What I am saying is that the idea of race is much more nebulous, mysterious and unquantifiable than materialists, Darwinists and genealogists would have you believe.

Biology is not the primary determining factor of your race. Race is also something you feel. It is not only your biology, but a set of beliefs, worldviews, feelings, thoughts, social agreements and actions that determine your race. It is your ethnos. You can change your ethnos, which is a shared language, a shared geospatial territory, a shared belief in a particular origin, and a set of customs, manners and outlooks. If you move from one place in the world to another, and you adopt all of these things for yourself, if you think and speak in the new language, believe what they believe, do as they do, and live in their territory, you are now one of them. You have changed your culture, you have changed your ethnos. We call this assimilation. People do it all the time.

For more on this, read Alexander Dugin's *Ethnosociology*[14].

Now to complicate matters further. Winston Churchill was born in England, but by all accounts, his sentiments, his view of reality, his political and economic thinking and activity, were entirely Puritanical-American. Americans can be born in England. Ezra Pound, William Joyce, and Douglas Chandler were born in America but were clearly European in their thinking, their activity, and their views proving that Europeans can be born and raised in America. A Prussian can be born in Rome as well. Just take a look at Mussolini. Look at the black people who are born and raised in white communities. They aren't out in the streets committing crime or living the thug life.

While being born within a particular phenotype or haplogroup and being surrounded by that group may provide you with some initial dispositions toward certain ways of acting and thinking, those dispositions can be altered throughout one's life or throughout the history of generations. It may not be easily done, but it is possible through a combination of personal efforts and total immersion.

Race is something you have and express. It is an unquantifiable recognition in your soul. It is not something to which you belong; in fact, it belongs to you. It is a qualitative difference, not a quantitative one. Skull shape and skin color are only minor factors and are as unimportant as any other materialistic phenomenon. Ethnos comes from the cultural spirit to which you adhere. A new term has been adopted in the 1990's to describe this. You may hear it referred to as a cultural Oversoul. The Oversoul which you feel and express and to which you attune yourself provides you with your race. To the extent to which your thinking, feeling, speaking, willing, and acting is in accordance with the impulses of that Oversoul, you have that race. This can actually change in an individual's life. Through spiritual awakening, emigrating to a new land, through conscious choice, being surrounded by a society of a particular High Culture, and the intensive and deliberate assimilation to that culture, one can have a new race and give up the old one.

In the part of America in which I live and the type of community it is, there are many different people descended from various parts of the world, but we do not segregate ourselves like they do in the big cities. We live amongst each other. We are all close neighbors and friends. And while we may have differing political and economic views, different specific goals in life, different religious beliefs, we would never consider each other to be cultural outsiders, others, or enemies. Never could we imagine being each other's object of war or conflict. It is unthinkable. We have barbecues and pool parties. We go kayaking together. We teach each other's children in school. We play recreational sports together. We work together. We produce artwork together. There is a harmony and coherence here that we feel intuitively. We have all assimilated to the American cultural spirit, such as it is.

Now, the American Oversoul is hardly an extant recognizable thing. It is barely a fetus gestating in the womb of history. It is a zygote floating in the ether. The American High Culture will be born roughly 2000 years from now (around 4000AD) and its characteristics are almost entirely unknown at this point and can only be theorized. What people think of as "American Culture" today is anything but. It is not the expression of the unborn American Oversoul. It is merely a combination of the amputated gangrenous limb of English capitalism, the twitching corpse of Puritanism kept in a simulation of life by artificial electrical zaps, the senile old cat lady of European liberalism, and a confused hodgepodge of ethnic enclaves separated from their origins who have more pride in the countries from whence they came than in the one in which they live. These phenomena will die out within a couple of centuries. But this is a story for another time and is not the subject of this chapter.

However, continuing my personal example, we as individuals are the cells of this fetus gestating in this womb and feel at ease about it in the rural setting in which we exist. Again, the crime and intercultural conflict occurring in the big cities is a phenomenon caused by the economic and political pressures that are magnified and exacerbated there by poor living conditions, propaganda, poor education, criminal conspiracy, the existence of unassimilated ethnic enclaves, and adherence to outmoded ways of thinking which are compounded and reinforced by close proximity to many people and tight links of communication networks and social reinforcement characteristic of large population centers. These artificial problems are more easily ignored, managed and solved in places where our alarm clocks are the morning gales and our pastime is gardening and our nervous systems are not overwhelmed or burnt out by external stimuli.

But anyway, I went to high school with many Jewish people and most of them think and act like Aryans despite the mentalities of their grandparents. One of my Pakistani friends that I've known since I was born wears flannel shirts and goose-down vests, owns a horse, and listens to Willie Nelson. He is more American than me.

I also know plenty of white people who grew up to work on Wall Street and at other banks and law firms and in the government and are thoroughly dedicated to perpetuating 19th century ideas, policy and economics to benefit therefrom much like the Jewish culture-distorter. These white people are Jewish in their hearts although they have not a drop of Jewish blood in them.

This is why the adherence to materialistic biological racial theories professed by both the left and the right and expressed in their desires for segregation and the Balkanization of America will ultimately fail to solve our problems. While the fragmentation of Balkanization and tribalization are likely imminent, unavoidable, and will provide a great deal of benefit, they are not the fundamental solution. They are likely a step in the right direction, but are merely a stop gap for the real solutions. A deeper examination of ourselves is necessary.

Balkanization and tribalization may solve some material problems such as problems with demographic conflict and crime and the enactment of more sensible local laws and ethical economic systems. They may create and protect the aesthetic type of person you wish to see born into the world. They may preserve certain superficial aspects of culture like diet, clothing style, art forms and erotica. And these may be some great benefits to creating ethno-states. But there is a fundamental problem here. If my Pakistani friend was forcefully kicked out of this region and moved to another region where all the West Asians and Arabs are meant to live, he would be miserable. He would be unwelcome amongst them. He would be a total alien to them. He doesn't think or act the way they do.

And let's say all of the Jewish people were put into their own region, and a particular white region is now empty of them. What about all of the white people still living there who adhere to economic thinking, capitalism, communism and libertarianism? In other words: all of the white people who act like Jews? What is to be done with them? And what about the Jewish people who think and act like Aryans and provide benefit to that culture? A locality would be kicking out the artists, thinkers, and workers who are spiritually Aryan and that culture will now be weaker and lesser for it. They would kick out all the blacks, even the ones who think and act like Aryans, and force them to live in communities where they feel unwelcome and unsafe. At the same time, they would allow culture-distorters and parasites to remain living in that region simply because they are white.

Wouldn't life be so simple if every friend was blond-haired and blue-eyed and every enemy was dark-haired and brown-eyed? Oh, how easy everything would be. But only an idiot fails to see that life is far more complex than that. People who see things in this simplistic immature way want fast easy solutions so they can benefit from them now. It is selfishness, laziness, cruelty and shortsightedness. They would kick out all the Jews but then realize that they themselves are still utilizing capitalist economics and outmoded financial devices. They still desire the acquisition of wealth; gaining money is still the highest goal of their life. They still believe in voting rights to secure their own selfish political gains. They will continue to lobby and bribe politicians to serve their economic and religious interests. They will still loan money from banks at interest and engage in usury. Many of them will continue to believe in the Jewish mind virus known as Christianity. They will have exiled all of the biological Jews only to realize that they themselves are spiritually Jewish, perhaps not in their overt religious form, but in every other way.

Such people are spiritually weak and impotent. Pathologies only affect weak organisms with poor immune systems. Culture pathologies are the same by analogy. One falls for the tricks of the culture-distorters because they cave in to social pressures, desire wealth, or fall for extortion tactics. One takes out a student loan at interest because they were pressured into ascending the bureaucratic status pyramid instead of imagining and choosing a different, more honorable life. One takes out a loan at interest to start a business because they desire wealth or fail to see another way to secure their economic needs. They fall for these tricks because they are weak and selfish. They do not follow a strict code of conduct rooted in spirituality. They can blame the system all they want, but the system exists because they endorse it hoping to one day become rich. They would never undermine capitalism so long as they hope to be rich one day or believe in the Puritanical work ethic which is the hallmark of capitalism, communism and libertarianism.

Our leaders can make positive changes, but the leaders come from us, and are just as weak as the rest of us, and we become blinded by money and power once we start making headway toward leadership. When we are finally in a position to make the change, we either decide not to follow through because we are suddenly wealthy thanks to our leadership position and we become pacified by wealth, or we are surrounded by conspirators who threaten and coerce us to the extent that we don't follow through, or we are assassinated by the people who benefit from the current order of things, sometimes because our security team was bribed or coerced seeing as they are generally weak-minded mercenary types and not loyal warriors in this Age.

Our problems are spiritual in nature and require a spiritual solution. We must stop loving money. We must become incorruptible and immutable. Accept no bribes. Fear no threats. Bend to no coercion. We must cease with this pursuit of individual happiness, this every-man-for-himself nonsense and have a sense of responsibility for the culture in which we live and a sense of honor and propriety over our own lives. Stop falling for the tricks of the culture-distorters. Neither a borrower nor a lender be.

Recognize usury as a crime and neither take nor give loans at interest. Do these things, and the culture-distorter will have no power here. The only reason the distorter does what he does is because he thrives in liberal, democratic, economic-oriented, capitalistic and communistic societies. So long as you have liberal, democratic, and money-oriented beliefs, you are also a culture-distorter. Your biological race has little to do with this. This is simply your spiritual orientation. Do you believe in outmoded, outdated, senile 19th century ideas, just like the culture-distorter whom you wish to exile? Or do you seek to get in touch with your Oversoul, your High Culture, and discover the current Spirit of the Age and live by those principles? You will find the Spirit of this Age is anti-money and anti-democratic.

If you lack spiritual discipline, self-awareness, and self-control, you will be taken in by ideologies. Any ideologies. You will believe whatever smarter men than you tell you to believe. You will believe in nationalism, materialistic racial theories, capitalism, communism, democracy, libertarianism, constitutionalism and so many other things because they sound nice. They sound like they will solve your problems on paper. But these ideas are old and tired. The 20th century has defeated and disproven them. They are corpses that have already been trampled under the march of time.

The social and political movements who live by these outmoded ideas and seek to establish them are akin to necromancers raising the dead to do their ineffective bidding. You will only notice that after you have quieted your mind and looked within yourself to your innermost truth, the core of your being. The pure unconditioned mind sees clearly. Your conditioned mind is polluted with ideologies created by other people. Your conditioned mind caves in to social pressures and desires. Only after radical mental purification brought about by self-awareness, emotional control and spiritual discipline will you begin to see reality the way you are meant to see it; from a higher vantage of calmness, clarity and truth. Then you can creatively act toward better solutions that call upon the strengths and talents unique to yourself. Only then will you find what you need to do in this life according to historical necessity and your place in this history, unpolluted and immune to the coercion that comes from other people and their interest groups.

Only then are you able to make political decisions or protect those who do. Only then can you sentence other people for crimes. Only then can you make real lasting cultural change and advancement. Anything short of this spiritual transformation and mental purification and you will remain ruled by emotions and subject to culture distortions and you will support ineffective political and economic theories which will only prolong or exacerbate our problems.

Kicking people out of your homeland wholesale based on what you believe about race and not what race actually is in spiritual fact may solve a handful of problems while causing a few new ones. If you want to kick out the culture-distorters, that is completely fine, just make sure you understand how to identify one. Their biology may have very little to do with it. It would be a shame to kick out our friends just because they look different. And it would be an equal shame to allow culture-distorters to live amongst us simply because they come from the same genetic stock as us.

Keep your head and heart clear, tread wisely, and do not get swept up in hatred, vengeance, the mob-mentality, or containment and controlled opposition deceptions. A superior culture for our future requires a superior form of justice rooted in spiritual knowledge and perception. A mature leader knows that there are no quick and easy answers to the problems and culture distortions which plague us. Begin with yourself. Be incorruptible. Eliminate any and all culture distortions and pathologies within yourself so you can better recognize them in others. Judge yourself before you judge others.

VII

<u>Governing and Non-Governing Elite</u>

The elite are not only the people who rise to political power and create laws. Those are the governing elite. There exist also the non-governing elite – those people who generate ideology not only through statecraft, oratory and military expeditionism, but through art and sagaciousness (or in a cruder sense, through propaganda and theory generation.) A small number of painters, musicians, filmmakers, sculptors, poets, authors, holy men, priests, mystics, philosophers, and other similar types can form the class of the non-governing elite – what Francis Yockey referred to as Culture-Bearers[4].

Let us refer back to the iron law of culture generation. A great individual generates ideology which enables the creation of laws. These laws then create the culture. Any person capable of generating ideology which has the potential of being widely adopted due to its capacity to successfully fulfill spiritual, social, political and historical needs for a people in a given territory can be said to be a member of the elite – specifically the noble elite known as The Aristocracy.

Of course, there are people who are capable of generating widely adopted ideology which does not provide for the needs of a people but instead inverts their needs and subverts the culture bringing cultural distortions, pathologies and ruin to a society. While these people may wield the power of the elite, they are not members of The Aristocracy. They are pretenders and usurpers – the corrupt elite – and history has shown that their power is temporary and based on repression and deception, not harmony or truth, and they are eventually brought low due to the fact that they are generally illegitimate. Although they do tend to find their way back to power era after era; tenacious and resistant weeds in our garden that require constant plucking and pruning.

The Aristocracy are the best of us. Today, they tend to be janitors, poor musicians, adjunct professors, suppressed politicians, censored thinkers, and cardboard box dwelling vagabonds. Our caste system has been so thoroughly inverted and perverted over the last few centuries that The Aristocracy has been relegated to the fringes to such an extent that they can hardly be said to exist in any visible or influential capacity except in rare and exceptional cases. The corrupt elite gained such an increasingly powerful foothold in our society beginning in about the Fourteenth Century that when the Age of Revolution came, such little trust was placed in the governing and non-governing elite that The Aristocracy was indiscriminately lumped in with the corrupt elite and all fell to the guillotine, the assassin's blade, the revolutionary council's judgment, the democratic impulse, the businessman's sabotage, the censor's redaction, the gossiper's venom, and the certifier's red rubber stamp. Such skepticism of power arose within the hearts of the masses that anyone who had the audacity to hold illiberal views, to display excellence, to think and act contrary to the mainstream, to uphold hierarchy, to believe in greatness and difference was shunned, exiled, imprisoned, assassinated, silenced, barred from holding office, disallowed to work, fired from their job, blacklisted in their career, had their works banned, unpublished, or rejected from publication, and found themselves with very little social selection, political access or financial stability. This is how The Aristocracy vanished from public view and is currently repressed to this day.

Today, our corrupt non-governing elite are Hollywood, pop stars, university professors, post-modern artists, compromised priests, delusional and insincere spiritual teachers, social media influencers, sociopathic grifters and ideologues and the secretive groups, non-government organizations and intelligence agencies who generate the theory which they all promulgate almost invariably. Most of the so-called "counter-elite" are merely containment and controlled opposition organized by and working for these self-same entities. Controlled opposition acts as a pressure release valve for the frustrated or a corral into which they can all be diverted, herded and rendered safe, ineffective, and non-threatening to the corrupt elite or used to carry out their agenda.

Another aspect of the iron law of culture generation is that The Aristocracy always exists no matter how repressed or suppressed they may be even unto assassination, incarceration and physiognomic degradation. The cultural Oversoul always manages to find individuals who are in tune with its impulses and are willing and able to express them. The corrupt elite know this and are always busy attempting to find ways in which they can cut the people off from their spiritual origins and connections by any means at their disposal including propaganda, coercion, brainwashing, pharmacology, technology, and so on. But for every Aristocrat who is brainwashed, blackmailed, DNA-altered or pharmacy-blasted into obedience, another one is born or twice-born to replace them. For every transhumanist they attempt to create, a purist will resist. They are the true counter-elite.

They have the choice of branching out in two paths: to remain the non-governing elite and continue promulgating sagacious ideology and art work or to enter the ring of politics and become the governing elite through regime change. (It is my opinion that regime change is necessary. Slow infiltration has failed. Individuals who go through the system with the intent of changing it from within are eventually corrupted, compromised, coerced, silenced or suppressed. The enemy is too overwhelming, entrenched and well-organized for a weakly bonded network of counter-elite statesmen, sages and entertainers to change it from within.)

Both paths, governing and non-governing, are noble and necessary although one path is considerably more dangerous than the other. A member of the non-governing elite has an easier time maintaining legitimacy as their ideas can change, they can retract outmoded earlier publications and modify their ideology according to their growth as thinkers without having committed sweeping overt cultural shifts on the material level which are much more difficult to undo. Their mistakes are ideational, and ideas can be changed with relative ease. Their battleground is the debate hall and there are (usually) no casualties in that arena.

On the other hand, the governing elite must act on the material plane and make impactful decisions that effect many people in very short periods of time. Small mistakes that result in material harm or misunderstanding can result in total failure and loss of legitimacy not only for the elite individual in question, but for the ideology which he promulgated. This type of setback can be devastating to a movement whose object is lasting and permanent regime change and positive cultural transformation. If a good ideology is subverted and undermined via mistake and misunderstanding, one to three generations must pass from memory before the attempt at regime change can be made again, and even then, the time will no longer be correct for that particular ideology as the cultural Oversoul will have modified its own impulses at least slightly. New theory generation must occur in the meantime and a wholly new preparation for regime change must be undertaken in accordance with the correct spiritual impulses appropriate for the changing times. Although the new ideology will undoubtedly be somewhat similar to the failed attempt, it will have key differences and its symbols and visible aspects must be entirely different to avoid association with the failed attempt which would re-trigger negative memories in the public mind and inappropriate links and correlations with undesirable and outmoded movements; although the old symbols should be remembered and honored for what they were as memorial pieces and to alleviate the unfair burdens of guilt placed on the descendants of those who waved those banners.

This is why it is of utmost importance for the governing and non-governing elite to work in tandem. They must act as a positive feedback loop of reinforcement and ideological modification and prevent each other from getting stuck in old ideas. The governing elite look to the non-governing elite for their speeches, their ideas, their vision, their direction, their communication skills, their symbolism, their spiritual discipline and connection. Without them, the governing elite would find their inspiration from the ghosts and corpses of the past and attempt to resurrect them which would be unsuitable for how the times have changed. Without the governing elite, the non-governing are impotent, ineffective, hopeless workmen without tools. They are voices without an audience of ears to hear. They are priests without a congregation. They are philosophers shouting at clouds. They are artists who starve to death and are quickly forgotten. Their ideas become delusional, unhinged and detached from reality. Their visions are untried and untested because the governing ones who would take their vision and run it through the friction of material reality – to try their ideas and determine whether they are applicable – are absent from their posts or uninterested in what the cultural Oversoul is desperately trying to express. The non-governing then attempt to modify what the Oversoul is telling them in order to appeal to or flatter the governing ones, or the masses, in order to gain traction and success in the field. This is folly of the worst sort and can only result in failure, corruption and decadence.

These two classes of the elite must be in constant communication and cooperation to keep each other in check and insure that the ideology, actions and laws are fresh, stable, appropriate for the times, in tune with the higher spiritual impulses, tested and vouchsafed, positive in their value, uncorrupt, actionable and effective.

The corrupt elite have these networks of communication and cooperation firmly in place. They know they must conspire together to succeed in gaining and maintaining power. It is easier for them to set their differences aside and work together due to what can be termed "mutual execrations." They are generally of a criminal sort and thus are able to blackmail each other. Each possesses proof of heinous crimes committed by the others. They allow this proof to be collected on themselves and dispersed amongst their co-conspirators as a form of trust and insurance, and this blackmail is held like a Sword of Damocles over the heads of the conspirators. "Cooperate or be sent to prison forever." This makes the undertaking of vast, far-reaching secretive conspiracies of corrupt governance not only possible, but quite easy. There may be no honor amongst thieves, but there are certainly many insurance policies.

There are other sorts of governing and non-governing elite types who can be said to be corrupt although they are not criminals but merely cowards. These types bend to the coercion and threats of the criminal types and engage in conspiracies either for financial, social or carnal reward or to avoid punishment and reprisal.

The Aristocracy does not engage in such dishonorable activity. If they did, they would not be The Aristocracy. They commit no heinous crimes and therefore cannot be blackmailed. Nor would they blackmail others due to the fact that they would not tolerate working with criminals. They also do not coerce because it is dishonorable and they do not desire to work with and support cowards or opportunists. So when the counter-elite wish for regime change, the organizing principle is much weaker and easily thwarted during a Dark Age when networks of power are more easily built through evil than through goodness.

Today, each Aristocrat has his own ideas of what is right, his own system of morality, his own religious beliefs, and his own code of conduct due to the fact that they have been suppressed and scattered for centuries leaving them bereft of a unified system of values to support their cooperative ascent to authority. Each wishes for all others who join him to believe the same and to possess the self-same views – that they possess the universal system of values by which everyone must live. Generally, he refuses to work with those who think differently from himself even though their goals and desires may largely align.

As a so-called "pagan" (an essentially meaningless title slapped onto anyone heterodox) I myself suffer this terrible reality at the hands of Christians. I am more than willing to work with Christians as our political morality is somewhat similar in the short term even if ultimately incompatible. Working together, we could achieve excellent political goals with which we both agree in a relatively short period of time, but they generally refuse to work with anyone outside of their faith. It must be their way or the highway – their memetic sophistry or nothing. They tend to be intolerant and uncompromising in this regard and are constantly seeking to destroy, undermine, and create enemies of "my" people. Blinded by doctrine, dogma, paranoia and their hatred of "us," they refuse to see our similarities and our potential to work as allies even if it is only for a few projects. This has shrunk the unified counter-elite's numbers considerably, although the overall numbers remain the same, they remain in obstinate disunion and internecine conflict.

In the modern United States, there are millions of Traditionalist "pagans" who are seen as the enemy of Christianity and therefore effective political action *en masse* is prevented from occurring due to the fact that Christians feel secure in their popular power as they wield the significant influence of their established churches and think tanks and are made arrogant by this small success rendering them blind to the pressing need to include Traditionalists in the greater movement of regime change. They believe that Christianity is the West and the West is Christianity - an obscene delusion ignoring the fact that the West is a bio-spiritual conglomeration of peoples that transcends any religion. They believe that their God-man is going to deliver them victory – a victory which is reserved only for the faithful within their peculiar religion and for no one else. They do not believe that they need to ally themselves with other groups to swell our chances for political success, firm in their belief that they will be spared apocalyptic suffering and will be rewarded for their faith after everyone who refused to convert is cast into the lake of fire and the world is magically handed to the true believers on a silver platter. For it is written. And that is all the proof that they need. So fearful are they of the failure, damnation, and ostracization with which they are threatened should they begin to think independently or when modifying their beliefs even in the slightest degree, they generally cannot accept anything as real, relevant or politically actionable that does not have precedent in or congruence with their old dusty book or the dictates of their church fathers. This is of course a generalization, but a large enough and true enough one to have affected significant political and social detriments to our society.

And to be frank, the pagans are little better. Considering Christians to be socially-engineered dupes and the historical enemy and oppressors of pagans – a position with which I agree and fully understand – they are unable to come to compromises as well. I have reached out many times with olive branches to the Christians and am willing to put aside my historical grievances with them, and every time I have done so, the Christians have considered it some form of satanic deception and refuse to create joint political alliances despite the obvious benefits while the pagans consider me some type of lukewarm traitor to their cause for even trying. This has demoralized and radicalized pagans and Christians against each other, and has radicalized the center against both, and understandably so; it is positively exhausting, and when compromises cannot be made after decades of attempts, radicalization is indeed the better option if a movement wishes for success. (The cold calculus of politics demands that if similar groups cannot unify, they will destroy each other so as not to "split the vote." This is also another case for fragmentation: instead of trying to reconquer a central authority, it might be better to mutually tolerate these different yet similar groups and create a multi-polar fragmented society and allow the central authority to perish.)

Not to mention: most people who refer to themselves as "pagans" are generally nothing more than spiritually unfulfilled liberals and feminists projecting their unresolved emotions, resentments and modernist political beliefs into homemade chthonic and telluric religions. They hate Christianity because they hold the bizarre belief that Christianity is somehow conservative and not liberal enough for their taste. Working with such pagans seems to be an absolute non-starter. The fear, hatred and conceit that wells up within these hags-in-waiting once they realize you are a Traditionalist and not some gay New Age Wiccan or liberalized-sanitized-pacified yogi betrays the absolute weakness of their character and impotency of their "spiritual" disciplines and renders them inappropriate political allies. They hear the thunder of Perun in your voice, they see the eye of Odin in your head, they sense the unperturbed invincibility of Shiva in your mind, they feel the pride of your ancestors in your heart and they witness their great enemy called Aryan Masculinity standing unbowed before them, their unvanquished foe, worse than the Christians. They become incensed at the human incarnation of the anathema of their political views and goals, the proof that they have not been victorious over you and they fear the potential for their undoing. They attack the

Christians with confidence because they are low-hanging fruit simple to vanquish – hypocrites with a history of contradictions easy to call out. But when they see the unbroken, unapologetic Aryan who does not bother calling upon any old symbols or systems but breathes with the Living Spirit, proclaims new possibilities for his people, moves in the brightness of the present and future of their vital pulsating blood, heralds the turning of the tide in their own favor, they see a true enemy, a true threat, an inevitable victor in whom they can find no hypocrisy or contradiction and they cower in fear while lashing out with impotent verbal venom.

This is merely one example of the inability of the aspiring counter-elite to organize across ideological lines. So many of the counter-elite aspirants fancy themselves leaders and great chiefs who possess the solutions for the restoration of the West and they desperately wish to keep that ideology as pure as possible even if it means failure to achieve short- and medium-term political goals.

It is my belief that widespread networks of communication and cooperation for the counter-elite on a national level is impossible at this time aside from the hidden militarist network of the Continuity of Government Program which is a tool that can be used for either good or ill and may or may not possess ideological legitimacy depending on who activates it and in what manner. The possibility existed in the 1930's for organic networks to develop but was squandered and thwarted. You may think me cynical, but it is my opinion that we must accept the fact that regime change will not occur at the large-scale national or federal level without some form of coercion, blackmail, war, or repression. And considering that a true Aristocrat would scarcely desire such options (even a true and noble Caesar would trigger an unfortunate civil war), we must accept the likelihood that the West cannot re-centralize under a new regime, but must in fact fragment into many small regimes which will be capable of maintaining their discreet ideological purity. It is possible that Europe may be able to unify, but it is highly unlikely that America can maintain its unity, and having lost its unity, it will be many centuries before re-centralization can occur, and it will occur under entirely new conditions and ideologies than any we can imagine today.

The only hope for the preservation of the Aryan peoples is to fragment into smaller sovereign political units and to cooperate with and be colonized and protected by the newly arising Slavic-Russian Civilization. This is in fact a form of fragmentation coupled with re-centralization: the ingredients for a true Imperium - different cultures united by common ethnos. Whether American, Irish, German or Russian, we are all Aryan.

VIII

<u>Fragmentation of Sovereignty</u>

The phenomenon of the fragmentation and centralization of power and sovereignty has been analyzed and explained by historians, philosophers, sages, sociologists and analysts of all sorts for thousands of years. We can find it in the Vedic scriptures, the poetry of Rumi and Hesiod, the satires of Horace, the book of the iChing, a spread of Tarot cards, the halls of erudite Russian institutes, the ravings of mad prophets, the musings of stoners, the observations of anthropologists, the petri dishes of microbiologists, the churnings of the ocean, the precession of the seasons, the comedies of Monty Python, the life cycles of trees, the radio telescopes of astronomers, the histories of kingdoms, the campfire tales told by elders, the data sets of sociologists, the coalescing and dispersion of art forms, and many places besides.

By now, it is a foregone conclusion that things split apart and come together and split apart and come together *ad infinitum.* The principle is intuitive enough, having a rhythm and logic that can be observed at all levels of nature. It would do little good for me to waste ink and paper re-explaining what wiser individuals than I have already adequately explained. What is left to us is not whether we split apart or come together, but the manner in which we do so. Do we split apart with war and antagonism or amicably and with understanding? Do we come together through repression and might or through commonality and shared vision?

We must recognize when it is time to split apart and do so gracefully. We must recognize when the season changes and it is time to come together and do so with mutual benefit. This is no easy task. There are times when groups want to split apart but the season is of togetherness. There are times when groups wish to remain together, but it is a season of dividing. Artificial union and forced division both end in tragedy. Harmonious union and symphonic division result in freedom and prosperity. But how does an Aristocratic elite class know when they are being artificial and coercive as opposed to being harmonious and symphonic?

This question cannot be posed to the corrupt elite because they simply do not care. They will force union or division based on what suits their selfish or cowardly interests and they are undisturbed by the deleterious consequences of their actions.

This question can only be posed to a conscientious Aristocracy who wish to maximize freedom, prosperity, security and wellbeing for their people within a given territory. During protracted crisis scenarios, a centralized elite cadre may ask themselves, "Should smaller polities be formed and sovereignty ceded to these diminutive units?" A decentralized elite cadre might ask, "Should smaller polities coalesce to form a federation and begin the process of centralization?"

Should…?

Such a strange word: "should." So packed with meaning, nuance, baggage, preference, ideology, expectation, hope, fear, moralism, belief, opinion, ambition and pregnant with potential conflict, potential celebration, potential disaster and potential victory. One man's should is another man's shouldn't. One man's imperium is another man's tyranny. One man's tribalism is another man's anarchy. Who is correct? Does the correctness of the position depend on the time it is proposed, being correct in one set of circumstances and incorrect during another? Does the correctness depend upon who makes the proposition, being correct when proposed by a culture-bearer and incorrect when proposed by a culture-distorter? Who is to determine who is who, which is which?

If I were to hazard a guess, I would say that both the appropriateness of timing and the appropriateness of person are required for the position to be taken seriously and acted upon. To gauge the level of appropriateness, a combination of analysis, historical sense, intuition, spiritual attunement, social responsibility, and cultural sensitivity are necessary.

Essentially, wisdom and justice must be found within the person making the proposition while historical precedent can be used to determine whether or not similar crisis scenarios were insoluble without either fragmentation (in the case of a unified society) or centralization (in the case of a divided society) and taking careful note of the consequences that came with either decision. Simultaneously, consultation must be sought with those who have fundamentally transformed their consciousness through the disciplines of an effective spiritual Tradition. They can determine for what the season is ripe like an oracle casting divination lots or a cosmic meteorologist diagnosing the spiritual weather. And finally, sociologists and anthropologists, and perhaps spy networks, must be consulted who have keen understandings and large data sets of the various groups composing the political units in question. What are their goals, desires, histories, feelings, attitudes, and so on? What is their most likely reaction given the chosen solution? Which interest groups and polities are compatible with each other? Which are incompatible?

This is all easier said than done and already presupposes a type of agreed upon system of evaluation, honesty, a code of neo-chivalric conduct and a unifying of scientific and spiritual paradigms. Cooperation of sympathetic personalities within the governing and non-governing Aristocratic elite across polity lines and interest groups is an *a priori* necessity for such a process to be successfully accomplished. Forcefully establishing and imposing such a system of values through educational institutions at this point in history might be seen as a form of tyranny and affront to the corrupt elite who would view it as a threat to their power and a confusing anachronism to the masses of people who are largely unaware of this historical necessity or doggedly subscribe to a pre-existing ideology with unwavering axiomatic adherence. An entire positive set of values must already be matured within the souls of the individuals who are to carry out such endeavors. It is my opinion that such an elite class exists currently and educating the masses to produce such personalities is not necessary. There are people who already possess courageously unconventional and holistic views of reality and the wherewithal to act upon such views.

We return to our "late bloomers," our true polymaths. They are scattered, unrecognized, alone, and leaderless, but they are here. They have always been here. Every generation produces at least a few for this exact purpose.

***

Will these individuals wish to re-centralize with a new elite cadre through regime change or will they decide to tribalize and Balkanize and redistribute the authority currently held by the federated polity? It is my view that at our current moment in history, the Europeans may wish to and be successful in a re-centralization through regime change. (Я смотрю на вас, Россия. Удачи. Вы – их единственная надежда.)

The Americans on the other hand may prefer to tribalize and Balkanize. Having achieved a pluralism of ethnoses, religions, ideologies, and goals not seen since the height of the Roman Empire, the centrifugal forces seem to be reaching the critical shear point of spinning the polities apart from their weakly concomitant cohesion. A nation composed of various pieces of amputated scion wood grafted onto a colonial trunk with no vital, territorially integral extant cultural Oversoul has little hope of remaining united.

There is a common saying amongst the New Right in the United States: "Social media didn't radicalize me. Crime statistics did." In my opinion, the New Right are not radical. They are normal. The vast majority of human history is characterized by Right Wing Traditionalism interrupted by short eras of Left Wing radicalism that disrupts the normal flow of life. It is radical to force multiculturalism onto a population that neither desires nor benefits from it. It is radical to ignore reality and impose one's wishful utopian thinking onto a world which will never accept artificial systems tyrannically replacing natural ones. Liberating oneself from all communal ties and responsibilities and all naturally inherited propensities and dispositions is radical. Endorsing, accepting, celebrating and protecting them is normal. It is radical to subvert and destroy organic hierarchy and replace it with chaotic telluric configurations of all sorts. Ordering one's life according to Cosmic Law and the proper balancing of polarities is not radical; it is the most natural thing a person can do. Ignoring clear and obvious dangers because it is illiberal to call attention to them is a surefire way of allowing your ethnos to be eradicated.

So what is to be done when there are diametrically opposed ideologies holding sway within one territory? Repress and silence the ideologues with whom we disagree, exterminate the opposition, and plant our flag as the new central authority and censor all dissent and coerce the population for eternity to maintain power over various interest groups who resent us? Or do we live and let live, split apart into smaller polities based on ethnos and ideology, go our separate ways, and see over time whose ideas, laws and culture are best suited to the wellbeing of human life?

I see three possibilities for the future of America. Tribalization and remigration (total fragmentation), Caesarism and remigration (re-centralization through regime change and partial tribalization), or technocratic tyranny and the eradication of human dignity (re-centralization through transhumanism and progressive liberal regime development.) The third option is what the current corrupt elite and their Left-leaning supporters are marching toward. It is their idea of progress and the logical conclusion of Liberalism. The Right wavers between the first two options.

The third option requires total repression forever in order for the central government, mega-corporations and the conspiracies who puppeteer them to maintain sovereignty. There will be such natural resistance emerging in every generation to such an unnatural state that it could only exist through abject totalitarianism. Liberalism has been a soft-totalitarianism since 1913 and has been rapidly becoming a more overt hard-totalitarianism as it approaches its apogee of desperation. As legitimacy wanes, repression waxes.

The second option requires some repression, but that repression would be aimed largely at non-white immigrants and criminals in order for the Federal government – which would likely need to be a dictatorship at that point – to regain its lost legitimacy under a savior king. The domestic white, Native American, black, and Pacific Asian populations would largely benefit from abject Caesarism although many would be moved around into different regions and would be forced to start new lives in new homes. Laws would be extraordinarily strict and discriminatory, but mostly logical and beneficial in the long term. Compromises would be made between a corrupt elite and a new Aristocracy creating an uneasy balance of power and many half-measures regarding remigration and criminal law likely resulting in civil war and precipitating option one within three centuries anyway. It is essentially the option for the "Last Hoorah" of the Federal government, and those who control the Continuity of Government Program infrastructure will likely attempt this option.

The first option requires an unknown amount of repression. It is the most chaotic, albeit likely the most desirable, option. Any repressions would originate within smaller polities, not from the Federal government (assuming they relinquish power without much of a fight being overwhelmed and rendered powerless by fragmented interests.) Large swathes of territory would be carved out based on ethnic and ideological lines giving Native Americans a chance to claim an enormous parcel of land, likely large parts of the Midwest and Southwest, to call their own. In this case, whites and Latinos would be remigrated from those areas. A large parcel of Southern land would likely be granted to the domestic black population. Whites and Pacific Asians would possess the rest and would likely intermingle without issue. The ethnoses who still have homelands in the rest of the world would likely be remigrated there. Any military conflicts would be contained to smaller belligerents with limited capacity for destruction.

How repressive, coercive or incentivized and amicable this would be remains incalculable and unpredictable. Judging this future scenario is like looking through a foggy window. Powerful corporations, transhumanists, militant foreign ethnic enclaves, Leftist radicals, religious zealots, aspirants to re-centralization and Federal restoration movements pose the main threat to amicability. Most other groups whose ideologies are less impassioned and whose differences from each other are less fundamental would likely need to defend themselves against these threats for a protracted period of time. Again, cooperation with and colonization and protection by the Russo-Slavic Civilization in the meantime (likely for centuries) would increase defense and survivability of the desirable political units.

IX

<u>Investiture of Sovereignty</u>

If sovereignty moves from one large central polity to several smaller polities and vice versa, then legitimacy must have a mechanism of distribution, selection, acquisition and investiture. This mechanism is entirely spiritual. Ignorance of this principle is the reason why civilizations tend to collapse during their scientific materialistic stage of life (what Sorokin refers to as the sensate truth system period[15]) or find it extremely difficult to transition to the next era. Having divorced spirituality from politics, economics, epistemology, and social institutions and having suppressed irrationality in favor of rationalism, elite aspirants will utterly fail in achieving actual legitimacy and thereby will not be sovereign – at least not for very long – and political and social problems will be magnified and exacerbated by the chaos and inefficacy of having an illegitimate elite. Deriving illusory legitimacy from things on the material level of reality through financial acquisition, written law, rhetorical displays, commission of acts of violence, bureaucratic maneuvering, moralistic appeals, token acts of magnanimity, favor-currying, technological applications and by undermining other people as to appear

Aristocratic by comparison but not in fact – being unable to actually rise to the spiritual level of an Aristocrat – the corrupt elite, or even honest elite aspirants climbing the ladder through "sensate" means, have no hope of maintaining power without bribery, deception, delusion and repressions of all sorts.

The only sovereign who can be said to be such without need of repression, deception, or coercion of any kind is that one who has earned and received the spiritual chrism of leadership. A true sovereign possesses legitimacy as naturally as his lungs possess air. He wields authority as naturally as he moves his own hands. The sovereign has wisdom earned from a life deeply lived. The basis for their sovereignty is irrational. It cannot be quantified or qualified rationally. There is nothing at which someone can point and say, "Here is the basis of their authority." It is not a credential earned at a university. It is not a ledger of financial transactions. It is not knowledge of secret handshakes or the degrees of a fraternity. It is not a number of votes in a ballot box. It is a life built on the Axis of the Sacred and the nature of that very axis is irrationality itself, without which, the Sacred becomes mundane and comprehensible and loses all true power. In fact, most of what is comprehensible to the intellect cannot be Sacred, and most of what is Sacred cannot be comprehensible; therefore, what constitutes the foundation for sovereignty is generally incomprehensible.

It is for this reason that liberals, rationalists and those skeptical of spirituality despise true hierarchy. It makes no sense to them. It is why their political theories of the last two and a half centuries have come to nought. They cannot quantify or qualify why one man is deserving of power and another is not. And when a man does in fact, rarely as it may be be, ascend to authority and sovereignty with the support of a critical mass of people who feel his chrism of leadership and intuitively (e.g. irrationally) understand the basis of his legitimacy, and this man stands outside of the mainstream paradigm holding views which are contrary to the current "truth system[15]" in place, the rational establishment and their supporters are overcome with fear, confusion, indignation, and shock being witness to a political advent which by their dogma should have been impossible. But the irrational man is not surprised in the least, understanding that reality is not as quantifiable as some may believe. He views the event as a sign of the times, the churning of the ocean of milk, God reaching His hand down and "stirring the pot" to shake loose calcified and rigidified systems and ideas.

There is very little rationality in the myths of King Arthur, Romulus and Remus,

Rama and Krishna, the Nihongi, the Sagas and Eddas, or any other foundational meta-historical narrative, but they form the very lifeblood of the laws, views and actions of entire cultures. Who is more worthy of aspiring to political power: the young man who spent his youth contemplating and playing out the legends of King Arthur and his order of chivalric knights and his adult years failing financially because he was seeking deeper meaning in life and was uninterested in money; or the young man who spent his youth contemplating Marxist and Keynesian economic theory and atomic physics and his adult years trying to maximize his monetary income?

One of these men feels righteousness and courage flowing through his very being with which he was endowed by the spirit itself, enabling him to act decisively to protect a maiden in distress or to support his brothers in arms or to vanquish an unbowed foe or to arbitrate a conflict. The other merely thinks about how to solve technical and sociological problems with unproven scientific and political theories considering human beings to be little more than rambunctious machines which need to be managed.

Only an "educated" rationalist would consider the theorist worthy of leadership when in fact he is only worthy of advising a real leader in limited capacity according to his intellectual acumen and the specific issue being examined.

Rationalists, seeing the world as a problem to be solved, prefer to be ruled by experts. Everyone else, seeing the world as an experience to be had, prefers to be ruled by rulers. It is the end result of rationalism to create a technocratic world order where absolute authority is given to experts, scientists, and sociologists utilizing cybernetic and behavioral theories to outlaw independent thought and manage the human machine. A more soulless, deleterious and undignified regime can scarcely be imagined.

It is irrational to be ruled by the man who grew up running through the forest with a wooden sword protecting his sister from imaginary orcs and dragons, yet most people would naturally prefer him to the stuffed shirt who can rattle off the fifteen most popular economic theories of the Nineteenth Century. Naturally the specialists have their place, but it is not one of leadership.

It is irrational to be ruled by the man who has dwelt in poverty and in sympathy with those who suffer in darkness and loneliness since his interests brought him into the depths of life instead of the workforce or the business meeting, and yet he is far more trustworthy and endearing than the man who holds his wealth as a sign of anointment, intelligence, and skill.

Specialists do not have good sense. So blinded are they by their field of interest, they fail to view reality holistically. They are unable to perceive the connections between disparate phenomena and therefore cannot grasp the science of government which must include all things which connect to and effect all other things. Only a generalist can appreciate the interconnectivity of all phenomena and can make sensible political decisions that have far-reaching benefit without the myopia of specialism.

The one who has placed himself in the non-moving hub of the wheel of life is instantly recognized as far wiser than the one who is further along the spokes nearer the rim. The ones who spin and whirl and go up and down with the vicissitudes of life may be famous, rich, clever, popular, crafty, and necessary for conventional life to continue, but they are not regal regardless of their desire to be perceived as such. The one who knows and can confidently say to these people (only the ones who pretend to royalty and leadership, for the ones living modestly beyond the unmoving hub are of a noble sort), "What you chase is illusion. What you desire is unimportant. What you do is vanity," and adequately explain why it is so from the vantage of the ageless wisdom of the immovable center and truly lives by this wisdom is the only one who can be said to deserve authority in matters of politics and spirituality. Everyone else in the political and spiritual spheres will be attempting to fulfill their own private ambitions, secret desires and delusional socio-political theories. The one who is centered on the Axis of the Sacred is the one who cares little for his own needs and is fully capable and deserving of wielding power with fairness, truth and restorative efficacy.

***

The attitude of such a one is recognizable by its characteristic synthesis of the transcendent and the mundane. There is a Zen koan, a paradoxical statement that must be meditated upon for its full meaning to be revealed in an experiential unfolding, that conveys the perceptual framework of a person who has transformed their consciousness at a fundamental level.

"First there is a mountain, then there is no mountain, then there is a mountain."

First there is perceived the phenomenal world, then there is perceived the causal world, then there is perceived the phenomenal world again with its causes better understood. This explanation is of course inadequate due to the fact that koans can never be fully explained comprehensibly, hence why it must be realized experientially. However unsatisfying, this explanation is warranted.

Most spiritual practitioners achieve the "…then there is no mountain…" stage and stop.

They believe they have achieved enlightenment, moksha, samadhi, nirvana, heaven, pleroma, liberation from conditioned reality. Their spiritual experience is then ratified as a dualistic worldview, one in which the material and spiritual worlds are separated by a gulf and the spiritual world is preferable. I call this "The Gnostic Delusion." Dualism stems from the hearts and minds of demoralized people with escapist tendencies or those who are easily satisfied with the achievement of inner peace and go no further. They view the world as fallen or evil, or at least ruled by evil. They see the futility of society and its goals and obligations. They believe political authority is inherently evil or serves evil. They see through the illusions of money, organized religion (in some cases) and politics and believe that the best way to beat the game of life is to not play it at all. They hypnotize themselves into complacency with their lot in life. Dwelling in the calm silence of samadhi, they tell themselves that everything is alright, they are happy as they are, they do not need or want anything, the world is as it is, I do not care. This is in fact an important stage in one's spiritual development that helps one cultivate a mind of equanimity toward all things of the phenomenal world and the unperturbed acceptance of their eventual death – but it is just that: a stage.

Most people believe that this is the highest perspective and there is none higher or more spiritual. In reality, it is an exercise, a period of chrysalis and death before a rebirth. The unfortunate thing is that most stay dead in this transcendent cocoon and never achieve the exalted heights of further spiritual development, seeing nowhere higher to go and having been totally emotionally pacified. Emotional pacification is not enlightenment. The eradication of the personality and the mystical merging into the universal oneness is only a stage before the creation of an entirely new personality – it is not the goal of spiritual practice although it is often mistaken and taught as such.

Tell me, if you were truly renounced from the world, why would you care whether or not you are renounced from the world? If you were truly enlightened and beyond suffering, why do you avoid your responsibilities as a human being? If the world truly is similar to a dream or an illusion, then why do you hide from living it? Why not fully engage with the dream? What is the difference between full engagement or complete detachment to a person who is truly renounced and unperturbed? If you are fully enlightened, why do you still have preferences and aversions?

Like an alcoholic who has not had a drink in twenty years because he is afraid of relapse, he is still controlled by alcohol. A renounced spiritual practitioner who remains disengaged from the world long after he has accomplished his conscious transformation is still controlled by the world and in fact not renounced very deeply at all, nor is his conscious transformation complete. The truly enlightened man feels no difference between war and peace, yet most spiritual practitioners are deeply disturbed by war and desperately crave peace. The enlightened man has no preference for activity nor non-activity and is neither active nor not active nor not not active. However, most spiritual practitioners prefer non-activity and boast of their disinterest in the world as though it is some virtue, a sign of lofty spiritual status and heightened awareness. Or if they are interested in some activity, it is usually as a peacenik lamenting the state of geopolitics who spend their time demanding or persuading that the world become more peaceful immediately so they can go back to sipping their tea and sitting on their comfortable cushion without worrying about how unpeaceful the world is. They correlate an increase in pacifism with an increase in spirituality.

When one achieves the "…then there is no mountain…" stage, one must not fall into complacency, becoming addicted to the peace and silence of samadhi, but one must continue to endeavor for self-awareness though there seems to be little or no self of which to be aware at this point. The self which disappears at the state of liberation is the conditioned self. The unconditioned self is still there to be discovered but can only be reflected upon by one who perseveres with their spiritual disciplines and allows them to unfold and change. Their original practices which brought them to this juncture will serve them no longer as they are entering the causal realm, the pre-conditioned realm, and, therefore; the new practices and perspectives which they must adopt in order to continue the spiritual journey cannot be taught to them by any teacher, priest or guru but must be discovered on one's own. There is no literature in existence regarding this fact. It is a deeply held secret, not because it is a secret, but because explanation and description past the point of the conditioned intellect is impossible and any attempts are almost always misunderstood and, shall we say, "unappreciated" by religious institutions. Formulating and promulgating advanced self-awareness disciplines cannot be accomplished in the realm of comprehensible phenomena, so, perhaps to the disappointment of my readers, I will not attempt to do so here.

However, we can take note of the two types of potentially advanced spiritual practitioners. The first type is one who achieves a certain milestone and mistakes it for total enlightenment and remains disengaged from the phenomenal world of activity, viewing it as pointless and undesirable and having this perspective reinforced by most religious, philosophical and spiritual doctrine. They feel as though they have finished, they reached the goal. They do not defend Mankind from its enemies because they come to an agreement with them: "I have awoken from your 'matrix.' I will leave you alone if you leave me alone. Do what you will with the NPC's. Just let me have my transcendent peace." (I'm looking at you, "schizo-maxxers," you modern Gnostics, Christians and Sufis, you New Age vibration-raisers, you lazy, thinly-veiled hedonists and nihilists. You have elevated your apathy and cowardice to spiritual heights. You may fool yourselves, but you do not fool me.) Being afraid of incurring bad karma or being sent to hell by their angry God for making political mistakes, they would rather preserve the purity of their own souls and remain inactive and uninvolved. In seeking Heaven, they seek their eternal endorphin rush no different than the transhumanists who would technologically and pharmacologically stimulate their brains to induce the same.

The second type achieves a higher transformation of consciousness and re-engages with the phenomenal world of activity according to what is required of him by his cultural Oversoul so that this Oversoul may express itself truly and fully, neither viewing it nor not viewing it as either pointless and undesirable or meaningful and desirable. He will act because he can and he is unperturbed. Whether he equips himself with rifle and blade to march forth to war, sits in his studio to make truthful if controversial works of art, literature, and theory, consoles and brings wisdom to the weary and confused in his temple or in the streets, or thunders his voice in the debate hall or theaters of politics, it makes no difference to him and he will do all this and more because he does not shirk his duty as a human man. He does not hide behind the arrogant pretense that he is above all this, that he has the correct beliefs; let everyone else suffer due to their lack of perspective, faith or discipline. Such spiritually pacified worms that belong to the first type are just as bad as the enemy, perhaps even worse, for they have abandoned their posts to return to their comfortable home afraid of fighting an uphill battle; feeling the sting of hopelessness, they allow the enemy to take ground without resistance.

In other words: when God comes to these spiritual practitioners and offers each the throne of the world in his turn, the first type asks, "Why bother?"

The second type asks, "Why not?"

Clearly one deserves political and spiritual power. The other deserves the oblivion that they so desperately crave.

****

The investiture of legitimacy occurs on this individual spiritual level and can be recognized in others by people who have earned and received the investiture themselves. Like recognizes like at this high level. Those blinded by dogma and doctrine who have not received any sort of spiritual investiture may see such individuals as mortal threats to their beliefs and therefore ultimately their lives. And perhaps rightly so in some cases as undesirable groups which go against the impulses of the cultural Oversoul of a given territory will become the targets of great individuals for suppression and remigration. Others may see them as the great individuals who they are: heroic personalities, wise holy men, and leaders worthy of their support. The division and fragmentation will occur on this level as the counter-elite arise, are recognized, and begin forming polities.

Cultural Oversouls that are young and vital tend to be quite ruthless when expressing themselves at a point where their territory, and therefore existence, is threatened. Like any organic creature, it will defend its territory and repel groups of people who belong to different cultural Oversouls that are not in harmony with itself. It will also cooperate with those Oversouls which are either symbiotic, similar or sympathetic to itself. A very young or fetal Oversoul that exists in a territory that is inundated with the disharmony of amputated limbs of other Oversouls will find itself in a precarious position and may need to rely on a more mature Oversoul which is sympathetic to it that will support and protect it.

For example, during the height of Ancient Rome, Europe was a loose conglomeration of tribes and tiny nations – their cultural Oversouls were either old and dying (in the case of the Celtic Oversoul) or infantile and vulnerable (in the case of the Western – or more specifically Anglo-Saxon Oversoul.) Rome extended its power northward through colonizing Europe. Some tribes fought this colonizing urge and others adopted it readily viewing Rome as a superior civilization and wanting to gain its benefits and protection. Those tribes and areas which were largely accepting of Roman rule became great and survived the collapse of Rome. These polities became the great cities of the West: Paris, Berlin, Munich, Prague, London, and so on. Rome planted its seeds, some European tribes behaved as foliated earth that accepted these seeds and the new Western Oversoul achieved its most potent expression in these places that were once Roman colonies.

Rome protected and fostered the fetal Western Oversoul, and in turn, the Western Oversoul gained wisdom and vitality from Rome, like the relationship of the adopted child with benevolent foster parents.

If America becomes the new barbarian conglomeration for the following two and a half thousand years, and Slavic civilization with its capitol in Moscow is slated to become the next great dominant culture by the 24th Century, living out its two thousand year lifespan that most cultures have to roughly the 45th Century, then it is in the interest of American polities in tune with the fetal American Oversoul to align themselves with Slavic destiny and political interests for the next twenty centuries. Polities which choose to side against the Slavic Civilization will eventually fail or be absorbed and integrated by the successful polities of the future American Oversoul.

Those who fought Rome lost. Those who sided with Rome were protected from local conflict and eventually became The West. You may hate Russia, you may obstinately believe that you are superior to them, you may believe they are uncultured, stupid, and are custodian of a collapsing economy, and every other rude and crude thing that Westerners and even many Russians and other Slavs believe, but it does not change the fact that they are the expression of the only young, vital, "fighting age" Oversoul in the world at this time. All cultural Oversouls begin in a crude and chaotic mode of life. To mistake birth pangs and adolescent chaos with decay and collapse is to be utterly ignorant of the patterns of history and the cycles of life. It is also arrogant projection. Westerners know and feel subconsciously that their society is dying so they desperately wish to believe that the entire world is dying, as evidenced by their fatalistic dementia which exhibits itself mythologically in the suicidal ideation of climate change despair and "post-apocalyptic" entertainment, sadistic I'll-take-you-all-with-me desire for World War III, Christian and New Age eschatology, and self-apportioned arrogant fear-mongering that the end of the liberal world order means the end of humanity itself and all that is good shall perish. Like a delusional old man who refuses to write a last will and testament, believing he will live forever and embarrassingly trying to hold on to what he once possessed and take it with him to the grave instead of granting it to the deserving youth, his selfishness results only in conflict and resentment from those who are younger than himself. (The collective West is suffering from "Boomer Logic.")

The South, the Middle East, and the Far East are husks of their former selves perhaps without even new zygote Oversouls. The West is old, senile and dying. America is in its zygote stage. The Slavs merely have to stake their claim and defend themselves from the zombie horde and the senile old man tilting at windmills. Now if only they could shake off the last vestiges of their Christian pretense and step boldly into their own future free of the Jewish mind virus, then their distinct historical mission will be properly advanced.

Get on the train, get hit by the train or get out of the train's way. To attempt to stop the train is unethical in the grossest degree being an affront to the spiritual impulses descending from the Cosmic Hierarchy itself. Not to mention; it is simply poor survival instinct. I leave it up to the individuals of the new Aristocratic counter-elite to decide for themselves and their own polities how they will stand in relation to the new Slavo-Russian Civilization.

In my view, we are the children of the West; we are not the West in the same way we are not our father. Our father is dying. We cannot extend his life artificially with an iron lung or by uploading his mind into a machine. It is unnatural. Let him die. Bury him in his uniform, wrapped in his banner with dignity. We must claim our inheritance from him before it is stolen from us or brought to ruin by other groups or squandered by his senile selfishness and dementia. Then we must ask our Slavic uncle for protection, guidance and favor in the hard times to come. I see no other choice for the great

American civilization which is to be born two thousand years from now. We need a long view of history and we must tend our garden very carefully at this early stage. We are the last of the West and the first of the Americans. Like a child cast into the wilderness, we will not make it on our own for our enemies are merciless.

X

<u>Hierarchy and Economic Will</u>

Those who believe in democracy fulfill their economic will with finance. Those who believe in Aristocracy fulfill their economic will with industry.

Democracy encourages and enables parasites who suck the cream off the top of the milk. Aristocracy encourages the milking of the cows and manufacture of the cream in the first place. This is one of the secrets of the Age of Revolution. The oversimplified version is that the merchant caste became corrupt and greedy and wanted to overthrow the Aristocratic caste. Tired of simply regulating a balanced economy, they desired to dominate the economy and unbalance it through speculation so that they may artificially inflate their monetary acquisitions and become financially rich even if it required the use of dishonorable tactics that would despoil the land and defraud the people. The Aristocracy (when in their noble and uncorrupted mode of activity) have little to no interest in finance and care only for the stewardship of their society and the land. To make a resource artificially scarce and drive up its price would be considered an affront against God, King, People and Nature. To give out loans at interest, causing unnatural stress on economic activity and fabricating money which does not truly exist using math equations and promissory notes causes debasement of the currency and reduces the people to debt-slavery. Aristocrats, holding legal, legitimate and divine authority, do not require money to gain or maintain sovereignty over a population of free people; not to mention, a Sovereign creates and owns the money of a given society and merely allows his citizens to utilize it and therefore cannot be bribed or coerced with his own assets. Only illegitimate usurpers require money in a bid to gain sovereignty over a population of slaves and a governing-elite who do not control the money supply.

Industry creates and maintains the necessities of life and stewardship. Finance merely purchases things which industry creates and maintains. It is ephemeral and less important. Aristocrats are interested in re-investing finances into industries and endeavors of one kind or another which improve the health, wellbeing, prosperity, freedom, and safety of a people and the beauty and fecundity of the land. A merchant caste which purposely neglects this responsibility so that they may ascend to wealth at the expense of the people and the land is corrupt and ought to be cast down to the earth as rapidly and mercilessly as possible. There are few things in the world more evil than the willful mismanagement of resources, for it is this mismanagement which precipitates a great deal of political, cultural, interpersonal and international problems. If you allow your mind to dwell for but the shortest of moments on the dealings and actions of the greedy bankers, financiers, speculators and businessmen, how many thousands of the most grotesque maladies, corruptions, catastrophes and sufferings can you discover caused by this web of evil that they weave, this cesspool of corrosion that covers our world? Indeed, these corrupt types are the very lieutenants of the enemy of humanity.

The Aristocracy, The Military, The Merchants, The Masses. This is the order of the natural hierarchy. To invert or displace the natural hierarchy of the caste system is to invite wreck and ruin to a society. If one wishes for sovereignty, one must become an Aristocrat. The other castes cannot gain sovereignty for themselves – not through revolution, finances, ideological modification, law or any other way whatsoever. Attempts to do so precipitate a vast array of problems known to history. Sovereignty rests only within the Aristocracy and nowhere else. This is not because they are tyrants; it is simply the natural way of reality. Your stomach does not have sovereignty over your brain. Your foot does not have sovereignty over your heart. It would result in dysfunction and death should such a change occur.

One is not placed in their caste by birth but by skill, dignity and vocation. The intersection among what one wants to do, what one is good at doing, and what is required of one by their community is a person's vocation; it reveals the caste to which they belong. Selfish thirst for political power is unbecoming. It is part and parcel of the democratic delusion and has no place in a dignified soul. Communal trust in each other's abilities and open communication of concerns and needs is the bedrock of stewardship and governance.

The degenerative process of the inversion of the castes is cyclical and common in great cultures. The first inversion comes when the Military wishes to overthrow the Aristocracy believing they can do a better job of governing. Perhaps they noticed decadence and corruption within the governing elite and imagine the divine investiture falling on their own ranks. This generally results in Prussian-style militarism and impenetrable bureaucracy. Next, the greed of the Merchants will encourage them to overthrow the Military. As noble character and divine investiture become less important, wealth is more desirable and is seen as a sign of anointment and a lever for control. Of course, the Merchants are adept social engineers, or are capable of employing adept social engineers, and they are generally successful in convincing the Masses that they should fight this revolution on their own behalf, that the caste system is being overthrown for the benefit of the Masses and not the Merchants. This is the ridiculous deception and delusion under which our modern West labors. An era of wars were fought between 1775 and 1945 and untold amounts of blood spilt to enthrone the Merchant. The communists and libertarians noticed this deception. The libertarians accept and endorse this and merely wish to make it known transparently that the Merchants are the rightful divine rulers of the world and seek to enter their ranks. The communists wish to achieve the final inversion over the Merchant placing the Masses as the rulers of society. With the tyranny of the proletariat, we would have The Masses, The Merchants, The Military and The Aristocrats in this completely inverted order of power. Paralleling the descent from a Golden Age down to the Silver, Bronze and finally the evil Iron Age, the hierarchy is scattered and brought to chaos, the Aristocracy is brought to utter ruin and their spiritual order suppressed almost totally.

Those who believe in democracy, money and the materialist scientific paradigm call this "progress." Indeed, if progress off the cliff and the progress of free-fall ending in the progress of being dashed against the rocks and the progress of the exsanguination of our bodies and the progress of our bodies becoming food for birds of passage is the type of progress one wishes to achieve, then "progress" it is!

Should the governing elite become corrupt, they should be recognized as no longer Aristocratic and they ought to be replaced by a counter-elite of true Aristocrats. The inversion of the natural hierarchy helps no one and is the social equivalent of a child throwing a temper tantrum. Imagine if a toddler replaced their parents with more toddlers. Social engineers and propagandists will generally take a crisis opportunity to present themselves or their clients and their "new" ideas as the proper rulers with the solutions to create a better world. The suffering masses, being desperate for solutions, increasingly angry, and generally uneducated in the realms of historical dynamics, divine investiture, and political science, oftentimes side with these scoundrels and loathsome parasites being deceived by their seeming lofty idealism. Thus begins the long march of decadence, decay, parasitism, corruption, slavery, debasement, and perversion – the deprivations of living under the tyranny of a shadow government of vile, hate-filled vampires who revel in your debauched state of life.

But how can one prevent or rectify the Age of Skepticism that comes to all cultures eventually? The time when divine investiture is questioned and more material and individual concerns begin to dominate is a chapter in the histories of every great culture. Perhaps it is natural and can never be prevented. Skepticism is a healthy step toward maturity, and the person who continues to learn and question and is truly skeptical of everything, including modern science (for can one call themselves a skeptic if they are not skeptical of science?), will eventually re-enchant their world with a newfound appreciation for deeper spirituality after their atheistic descent into particularity and searching for ultimate causes. Skepticism, taken to its full conclusion, leads one back to divine causes and spiritual enrichment at a higher level with hard-won wisdom and intelligence. It is when the skeptical period is artificially prolonged by parasites and distorters for their benefit that it becomes a danger. A return to spirituality on a cultural level would eliminate the power of money and the thrall it has over the minds of the people. When a culture's interest returns to the spirit, the economy is placed at a low level on the hierarchy, there merely to satisfy the needs of people so that higher cultural activity can occur.

Who benefits from spiritual ignorance, from materialism, from distrust in the soul, from toiling and tired masses, from unhinged and unwise technological progress, from myths of progress and linear time? Who benefits from the ideology that things must be bad now but will get better with time so long as you believe hard enough, so long as you allow current abuses and exploitation to continue, you will be delivered… one day…?

Only parasites who wish to feed off their host for prolonged periods would push such delusional ideology of progress and messianism – whether it is the messianism of a coming savior God-man or the messianism of a coming technological singularity or the messianism of the "end of history" brought by global democracy – it is a delusion that would have you wait and wait and wait for a future that will never come while the parasite continues to feed on you in your weakened state via debased economics. You would refuse to move against the parasite if you believe the messiah will save you from them. You would refuse to solve the problem if you dream of the day that the scientists and experts will solve it for you. If you just believe hard enough and long enough, you will be delivered a utopia where all diseases are cured, aging no longer occurs, and happiness reigns forever. Whether you are waiting for science, Christ, Kalki, or the racially and sexually ambiguous President of the World, you will wait forever.

This is why the West will likely fragment. The rekindling of a Golden Age, the reorientation of the proper natural hierarchy, the restoration of the true Aristocracy, can likely occur only on small scales where the members of a small polity will have a much easier time agreeing on what is to be done, what courses of action can be taken, how an economy can serve them best, how leaders ought to be appointed for their greatest good, how a government can be rapidly reorganized, new ideology promulgated and new laws written. The many interest groups which make up the Western conglomeration will achieve nothing but stalemate should they continue to bicker and compete within a central government. The stalemate and illusion of progress serves the parasites. Smaller polities which are not as severely influenced or hindered by culture-distorters will have very little problem coming to decisions regarding how to deal with such matters swiftly and efficiently.

Attempt to outlaw interest rates and usury on a national federal level and you will fail, likely by assassination. Attempt it in a small polity of say ten thousand people, and it will be unanimously agreed upon within minutes. Attempt to outlaw the gold standard and fractional reserve private banking and instantiate a true lawful fiat currency at the federal level and… well… cemeteries are filled with epitaphs which read, "Here lies a man whose final act was to stand against the banking cartel." But in a small polity, one could write a law that says, "Our money is worth this much because the law declares it so according to our ideology of what money ought to be. It is free from the illusory value of hoarded gold or promissory notes. Its value is determined by the necessary regulations of the Sovereign and the needs of his people and their land use." There are certain groups who would be very displeased with this form of true fiat currency due to the fact that it has been historically proven to eradicate poverty, toil and homelessness for the citizenry as soon as it is issued while simultaneously eradicating the power of the parasite, rendering him immediately criminal and utterly unfit to live within the Sovereign's territory lest they change to a more noble occupation befitting the newly adopted ideology and law. Certain mass exiles and remigrations throughout history begin to make more sense from this perspective. Was the cause truly hatred and discrimination or was it simply that there was not enough room in the prisons?

XI

<u>How Merchants Retain Power via Sabotage and Technocracy</u>

After the Merchant caste dispossesses the Military and Aristocracy, their chief concern becomes the maintenance of their stolen power. They begin by carrying on the revolutionary social engineering that disrupted the natural hierarchy and created the chaos that allowed them to initially secure power. This includes the creation of institutions and the infiltration of existing institutions to create and spread ideology that encourages wealth acquisition, economic thinking as the basis of epistemology and ontology, libertine selfishness, hedonism, positivism (in the Randian sense) to appeal to the culture-retards, communism to appeal to those who instinctively react against positivism (playing the Hegelian dialectic of controlled opposition), skepticism in virtue and spirituality, egalitarianism, feminism, scientific materialism, consumerism, critical and anti-structural ideations that are perpetual and insoluble, and ultimately transhumanism. Any alternative ideologies that originate organically from the counter-elite or the scattered Aristocracy must be attacked and suppressed in every way possible.

For example, social engineers push the belief that the only alternative to capitalism is communism and the only alternative to communism is capitalism, as though those two systems are not inherently the same, being based on the same principles of currency creation and economic thinking. (Communism may be the stage three cancer of society, but capitalism is stage one cancer. They are both going to kill you eventually.) Always be aware of the Create-The-Problem-Offer-The-Solution tactics of social engineers that act as containment, controlled opposition and diversion. This tactic can be found in nearly every field of interest to artificially divide people – particularly the Left and the Right – on problems that they would normally agree upon and solve together if only they were allowed to be educated on sensible alternatives.

Establishing the widespread belief that money is inherently valuable and that it represents status, freedom and power is the parasite's ladder to success, their ticket to the top of the social hierarchy and establishing their elite status as divinely ordained, correct, proper and acceptable. If the English Calvinists and Puritans invented this idea alongside their invention of capitalism, the parasites and culture-retards prolong and maintain the idea long past its expiration date. Many Christians and New Agers maintain the belief that wealth acquisition is a sign of spiritual advancement, heavenly favor and emotional healing while failing to understand or concern themselves with the diabolical mechanisms by which currency is created and the evil purposes for which it is taxed. As long as the Masses believe that they too can become rich, powerful and free through the acquisition of money, they will not begrudge their plutocratic and kleptocratic governing-elite too harshly, holding out hope that they may attain that same status one day and also retain it beyond reproach.

However, this is demonstrably untrue given enough time. The Merchant class, once in power, quickly begin to close ranks and write new laws that will insure only those who think and act like them will be afforded opportunities to gain wealth of any significant amount. Those who hold to honorable codes of conduct and spiritual tradition will find that they cannot or do not want to become rich no matter their efforts due to the evil nature of these new economic incentives, legal structures, and uses of tax. Generally speaking, barring exceptional cases, only those who are soulless, clueless, unscrupulous, anti-spiritual or dishonorable can obtain vast fortunes via today's laws and incentives.

After this spiritual and ideological glass ceiling has been placed over all of the honorable and conscientious individuals of a society, a further stage of the refinement of exclusion is carried out. Now ascent up the social hierarchy will be determined by race and sex. Since the conscientious and wise individuals are generally no longer part of either the governing or non-governing elite except in certain cases, most people in positions of power will not notice that this change is taking place, or noticing it, they will encourage it due to the fact that it may benefit their selfish goals in one way or another. Laws are written to artificially uplift newly-dubbed "protected" demographics of people who have historically been unable to ascend to positions of power within a given society; especially if that society is not their own. Of course it is difficult for foreigners to compete with the dominant cultural group and rise to positions of power and authority in a given society built by the dominant group's ancestors. Why should it be any other way? Why should anyone other than the descendants of the culture's founders or the culturally assimilated be the primary benefactors of a given society?

These simple questions are uncouth and distasteful to those who believe in multi-cultural progressivism as they have an *a priori* assumption that multi-culturalism is a moral good and mono-culturalism is a moral evil (seemingly only in white nations in this era.) It is a wonderful daydream and nice utopian wish to see everyone hold hands and sing kumbaya in the happy global rainbow coalition where we all have equal access to land and resources, but in the realm of politics and justice, we must deal with how human beings actually are in the real world – not how we think they ought to be in our imaginations. It has been discovered that social trust only increases in adolescents and most adults when interacting with members of their own ethnic in-group and decreases when interacting with an out-group.[16, 17] Human beings are born with innate in-group preferences. It is neither moral nor immoral; it simply is. To change this would require constant social engineering (a.k.a. brainwashing and coercion) which could easily be considered objectively immoral particularly if outcomes result in low trust and high crime conditions within a given society. When in-group members are still living in poverty, suffering and disease, why should special considerations be given to the out-group at the social, economic, political and spiritual expense of the in-group? Because a few sociologists in the 1960's convinced us that it was morally good? Because members of a particular religious persuasion operate on an apocalyptic belief that we must all aid and abet a particular out-group?

During the first wave of closing ranks, the most unscrupulous people ascend to the top of the social hierarchy and are almost invariably culture-distorters, culture-retards and parasites from a foreign diaspora or mobile short-term residency group not belonging to the host culture. Since they have no emotional, historical, familial, communal or spiritual connection to the host population (or have abandoned such), they feel few qualms in undermining, exploiting and debasing them.[18, 19] The first people to notice that this is happening will be the ethnic descendants of the founding race of the culture who continually maintain and renew their connection to the cultural Oversoul either consciously or unconsciously – the dominant group of people. In the case of the West, this would of course be heterosexual Aryan men who are first to feel the sting of being downgraded by laws and economic incentives that reduce their capacity to succeed in their own society. During this first wave of Merchant class rule, it may simply feel like misfortune that the dominant group is being downgraded, and they may grin and bear it in the name of "morality" and "equality" – values inculcated into them by the social engineers who exploit the Aryan's inherent compassion, fairness and social feeling. However, during the second wave of closing ranks, it becomes obvious that it is indeed a direct assault against their people.

When positions of wealth and power are exclusively granted to non-dominant demographics in the name of equality and morality by writing laws that enforce this equality by specifically preventing the dominant demographic from even obtaining these positions themselves, it becomes quite clear that these positions would seldom be earned by non-dominant demographics for any number of reasons both systemic and character-based. The positions must be granted to them via special placement programs or by exclusion of the dominant group and then legally protected from revocation. This means that non-dominant groups are not ascending the ladder of success via merit, skill, dignity, allowance or vocation in significant enough numbers to please the social engineers, so the dominant group must be attacked and prevented from obtaining these positions via bureaucratic, economic, social and legal exclusion. In order for the West to be "inclusive," white men must be excluded from their own society. White men are punished for imaginary crimes that they did not commit – including "thought crimes" – and for being born with their inherent characteristics, in the name of vengeance against Aryan ancestors on behalf of spiteful non-Aryans.

And how can one be angry with the members of the non-dominant demos who claim these opportunities afforded to them by the social engineers? It takes a special kind of dignity, wisdom and conscientiousness to decline ascent up the hierarchy out of respect for the host culture in which a non-dominant person lives. When an unqualified or unassimilated non-dominant gains a position that rightfully belongs to a qualified dominant or assimilated non-dominant (according to the views of the dominant group), the one who creates the reasoning behind the hiring decision is to blame – the NGO's, universities and think tanks and their members and associates who generate and promulgate ideology. We must never lose sight of the fundamental causes of our problems and mistakenly blame a scapegoat or take a swing at the low-hanging piñata. Reserve your energy for the true enemy and seek alliances with (or at least neutrality from) those who may actually be sympathetic to your plight even if unaware and taking advantage of it at first.

Exclusion of the dominant group and the artificial ascent of non-dominant groups has a twofold purpose that benefits the culture-retards and distorters. The dominant group will be economically, socially, politically and spiritually undermined and subdued, perhaps unto their complete disenfranchisement and destruction of their cultural forms, rendering them finally non-dominant, while struggling non-elite (the Masses) and counter-elite will fight amongst themselves and compete for dwindling opportunities and blame each other for their problems while the more secretive social engineers go unnoticed and unrecognized. It is both a direct assault against the Aristocracy and the other members of their ethnos and a diversion of would-be corrective revolutionary energy.

The Left has been given a memetic weapon from their social engineers to attempt a riposte when Aryan men notice their own plight: "When you are accustomed to privilege, equality feels like oppression," to which I answer: "When we are the ethnic and spiritual descendants of the founders and the dominant cultural group who continually work and self-sacrifice to maintain the civilization of our ethnos, we are more deserving of the benefactions of our society than others, and attacks against our group are exactly that: simply attacks against our group. We have the right to defend ourselves. Equality for the sake of equality is in fact oppression. No two things in reality are equal - our morality stems from this fact and we will not apologize for it or compromise against it."

The new Merchant rulers know that their greatest threat are the traditional members of the dominant group who instinctively feel a need to solve economic, social, political and cultural problems whenever they see their people suffering. If the dominant group remains within the governing elite, they may take corrective measures, write better laws and reconfigure the economy and other institutions to insure the wellbeing of their people even if it costs them wealth and power. A parasitical group would feel a pressing need to prevent this from occurring because the mechanisms of their wealth acquisition and power mongering would be eliminated. They will seek to downgrade, undermine, out-procreate, and even destroy the dominant cultural group. They can achieve this through mobilizing the vast resources at their disposal within their social engineering institutions: demonizing and demoralizing the dominant group, turning their women and children against them, turning other ethnic groups against them, and using pseudo-sciences like psychoanalysis and Critical Theory to "deconstruct" their views on life and claim that they are evil and problematic at a fundamentally cognitive level while erecting irreconcilable double-standards such as the foundational tenet of Critical Theory that it is fundamentally impossible for dominant groups to understand the experiences and views of non-dominant groups while it is very easy for non-dominant groups to fully understand the experiences and views of dominant groups. This is a reprehensible and dishonorable weapon used to great effect when attempting to persuade the intellectually unprepared to believe in perverse ideologies with which they would instinctively disagree. Wielders of such weapons ontologically deny the dominant group of possessing the faculty of empathy while claiming it solely for themselves. They simultaneously complain of being the victims of dehumanization while using the weapons of dehumanization. There are few mentalities and behaviors in existence as repulsive and disgusting as this.

This is where moral arguments may very well reach an impasse. Progressives will say that all of these changes are a good thing while the downgraded previously-dominant group will say they are an evil thing. From the perspective of a Traditionalist, it is objectively good to serve the needs of your own people, your own ethnos, first and foremost. The considerations of other groups must come only after every need of your own ethnos has been met for the full and complete self-fulfillment of your own cultural Oversoul. Meeting the needs of others who do not belong to your ethnos is a luxury that only fulfilled cultures can afford, and even then, only in very limited, controlled and carefully regulated capacity in order to prevent parasitism. Differentiating between those deserving of help and those who are merely exploiters and parasites is a finely tuned sense that only the wisest possess. From the perspective of a Christian or a progressive, the opposite is moral. To them, it is a moral good to indiscriminately help everyone else first even if it means your own undoing and destruction. A noble sentiment if you have escapist tendencies, a dualistic outlook, an aloof resigned attitude, hate the world and do not care about the future of your own people.

From the perspective of a cultural Oversoul – a culture's heart and brain – it is evil to allow the undoing and destruction of your ethnos in the same way that your biological heart and brain believe it is evil to allow your stomach to go empty or a disease to go untreated resulting in organ failure and death.

From the perspective of "being nice," it is a good thing to allow yourself to die so another may eat. Self-sacrifice may be very noble and spiritually appropriate in some cases and absolutely ridiculous and foolish in others. Would you sacrifice your life and wellbeing so that a tapeworm could continue feeding? Would you sacrifice the future of your own children so that an alien can feel more comfortable?

It is possible that agreement may never be had on this point. Some people simply view morality differently and there may be no persuading them otherwise in some, if not many, cases. Therefore, compromise may be a waste of time and energy. Always attempt compromise with your opponents first. It is noble and educational. You learn their needs and views and you express your own to them and you are afforded an opportunity to keenly and honestly examine how resources can and cannot be allocated. But after that point, you should have a read on who they really are and what they really want. Determine if they deserve your compassion or not at this point. If they do not deserve it, if they are attempting to deceive or exploit you, no compromise shall be made and no quarter given. Your laws, economics and institutions shall be configured and maintained to serve only your people and not theirs. You must be fully prepared for self-defense in such cases. This is the cold hard reality of politics – an arena in which moralism does not belong.

Although sovereignty moves, fragments and centralizes in many natural ways, it also moves in unnatural ones via treachery, moral conceit, and deception. One must cherish their sovereignty. It is a gift from God. Do not squander it in the name of "niceness." Your culture is ascendent because your Oversoul is more vibrant and vital compared to others whose time is past or not yet come. You are not required to "feel bad" about this. When you see someone bound in a wheelchair, do you break your own legs and sit in a wheelchair of your own so that you can achieve equality with them? Self-mutilation is a repulsive affront against what God has given you to achieve your self-expression. Do not allow pity and modesty to degenerate into humiliation and self-sabotage. Do not flagellate and damage your own body or allow others to consume it as a way to expiate your guilty feelings. God has granted your people power and ability for mysterious, perhaps unknowable reasons. Stand tall and be grateful for the capabilities which you have been granted and use them. To do less is to spit in God's face. The meek shall inherit the earth only when strong warriors defend them and this good earth from their enemies.

Legitimacy must be carefully cultivated and maintained with wisdom and reverence. Love for your ethnos is the bedrock of legitimacy. If you trade the wellbeing of your own ethnos for the sake of those who would exploit you and your people, for those who do not respect your Oversoul, your culture, who refuse to assimilate to it or assist in its fulfillment, you will see your legitimacy rapidly vanish and your sovereignty stolen by the unworthy, and your cultural Oversoul will succumb to the pathologies unless a more worthy Aristocratic elite reclaims it through great efforts, and your name will be marked in the histories as that of a great traitor, an example of reprehensible senselessness.

***

The specter of transhumanism and technocracy is another method, perhaps the final method, by which the Merchants, culture-retards and parasites attempt to maintain their power.

After the second wave of closing ranks and the previously-dominant group is largely disempowered, a counter-elite from within this downgraded group will attempt alternative

166

methods to gain sovereignty and power. They may invent alternative economic systems which benefit them, ideological generators that shift the culture, or "game the system" in other ways to climb and correct the social hierarchy. Seeing this, the corrupt elite will begin a more drastic way of "pulling the ladder up behind themselves" to prevent the downgraded group or any other counter-elite from achieving success.

There are attempts to re-write property law being made by using social engineering to persuade the masses that owning private property is deleterious to the wellbeing of the environment and the people and that property should be regulated by a group of scientific experts and a totalitarian regime who know better[20]. Of course, the corrupt elite already own most of the property in the world, so no matter how these "scientific experts" decide it should be doled out and used, it will in fact be rented out in one way or another (if not by money, then by social credit) by those who already own it seeing as they are the ones writing these "humanitarian and environmentally conscious" laws. They will prevent anyone from ever owning property and thereby destroy the ladder that they themselves climbed to the pinnacle of the social hierarchy while simultaneously uprooting a people's connection to the land. While the plebeians are out and about and "[their] living room is being used for business meetings when [they] are not there,[20]" do you think the corrupt elite living in their protected mansions are going to be sharing their intimate living spaces with others while they are off vacationing?

They offer these solutions to environmental and economic issues as though there are no better solutions, as though they are not the very industrialists and financiers who caused these issues. Permaculture has been the baseline subsistence for all cultures throughout all of human existence. New technocratic regimes and their alleged "solutions" are utterly unnecessary.

They will "expose" myriad problems with financial systems and law enforcement methods, demanding that all wealth be electronic, regulated and surveilled by computer systems, the infrastructure of which they own and control, and all people should be constantly surveilled in an attempt to prevent terrorism, violence, thievery, black market trading, human trafficking, environmental degradation and so on. The crimes that they commit and terrorize us with incessantly are constantly blamed on scapegoats and pazzis and used as justification for this totalitarian system. Aryan men, being an increasingly angry and bitter downgraded group and the most significant threat to the corrupt elite will be targeted by "crime-prevention" methods as can already be seen in murmur and rumor as the corrupt elite make the fallacious claim that "white supremacy" and "right wing radicalization" are the greatest threats to the safety of our nations. Being a traditionally oriented white man who loves his own ancestors and people is considered a threat to national security. (The jokes write themselves these days.) There are even social credit systems already put in place and are euphemistically referred to as "behavioral threat assessment and management.[21]" Instead of understanding and fundamentally fixing the social, political and economic issues that lead to anger, violence and revolution, they will simply identify people who they believe may commit violence and kidnap, medicate, brainwash and subdue them back into slavery.

Since the corrupt elite either do not belong to the ethnos which created Western culture or they are beholden to and serve these non-Aryan ethnoses or they belong to the class of culture-retards, they cannot hope to have any legitimacy and must rely on repressions to maintain power. Modern technology allows for such repressions as have never before been seen in recorded history. The hope of the corrupt elite is that their repression will gain a maximally effective apogee that will sever Western man entirely from his roots and his identity; that their goal will be achieved and the threat of an Aryan resurgence thwarted with finality.

Enter transhumanism.

Liberating oneself from God. Liberating oneself from communal religion. Liberating oneself from king and country. Liberating oneself from familial responsibilities. Liberating oneself from ancestry. Liberating oneself from gender roles. Liberating oneself from gender. These are the waypoints passed while cascading down the slippery slope of liberalism toward its final destination: transhumanism – liberating oneself from humanity entirely.

When identity is viewed as an unimportant social construct – optional and mutable, selectable and changeable, a fashion accessory for vain expressionism – identity becomes utterly meaningless.[22] One who believes in this selectability and mutability has hacked away at the roots of their identity and separates themselves from their ancestors. Actual identity is sacrificed in favor of belief-based identity. The Tree of Life is felled and crashes to the ground and in short order will rot and become home to maggots and mold.

The concept of transhumanism is quite vast and beyond the scope of this book, so I have already written a book entitled *Transhumanism and Contemporary Spirituality* where I bring to light the more hidden spiritual, paranormal, cognitive, political and sociological aspects of this ideology.

For those readers who are unfamiliar with the concept of transhumanism, in short, it is the application of materialistic science to alter the human being by grafting onto it elements from the mineral, plant and animal kingdoms. Through the application of genetic engineering, pharmacology, and biomedical technologies, certain researchers wish to "climb the Tree of Life" in a more materialistic, self-guided, rapid, and intensive fashion according to their own fancies of what a human being ought to be in defiance of what one actually is. Transhumanists are people who view humanity, suffering and death as problems to be solved. They are generally hedonists who fear death and wish to prolong life, maximize pleasure, and conquer the known universe in a material and utilitarian sense. They go beyond *negative selection* of biomedical therapies and modalities (bringing sub-normal human deficiencies to normal human functioning) and have moved into the realm of *positive selection* of biomedical modalities (bringing normal human functions to supra-normal capabilities.) The transhuman impulse is driven largely by the desire to take total control of the human condition, the human experience, into one's own hands and alter it to suit one's own preferences via non-spiritual means.

They imagine themselves with mechanical wings so they may fly, mechanical eyes which see beyond the currently visible light spectrum, sunburn-resistant skin so they may lounge on the beach or explore the untouched deserts, genetically modified livers so they may drink obscene amounts of alcohol, gills so they may swim the oceans, computer processors in their brains so they may crunch more numbers, and so many other fantastical capabilities besides. But what they will truly receive is soulless slavery to their own desires and bitter dissatisfaction with their ever-expanding and increasing expectations of life, not to mention the incessant competition with those who have more sophisticated modifications.

Whether the reader should morally agree or disagree with transhumanism is not the subject of this book. The precession of legitimacy and sovereignty is.

Transhumanism creates rootlessness; the condition of being aloof and detached from ancestry, humanity, identity, community and the world – the nightmare scenario of having a population not of people, but of genderless automatons with no lineage, of having babies born not of love and the union of opposites, but grown in technological vats instead of a woman's womb. A person who possesses no passed-down code of conduct from their forebears, no honor-bound connection to their family or ancestry, no motherly love, no fatherly duty, no brotherly strength, no sisterly femininity, no spiritual connection or continuity, no communal ethnicity, is a person who has no foundation for principled action or any cultural goal beyond self-satisfaction. In other words, it creates the perfect corporate employee or cog in a state machine – a non-human entity which can work on behalf of a slave-master while being flooded with endorphins and satisfied with daydreams. Meanwhile, the hopes of the slave-masters is that they will have fashioned a way in which they can live forever – either genetically, pharmacologically, or mechanically – becoming the perpetual incumbent governing elite. They will attempt to maintain as much of their own identities as possible while encouraging all others to destroy their own identities in order to eliminate their ethnic competition and end the cycles of the birth, life and death of cultural Oversouls – to insure that these Oversouls cannot exist within this world ever again. The earth itself will be reduced to a gigantic electrical device, a transistor in a circuit board, bereft of spirit, a sterile imitation of life.

Could such identity-less automatons ever possess sovereignty? Could such non-human, unmoored, unattached, discontinuous entities ever ascend to the Aristocratic elite and guide a culture?

Again, I leave this chapter with an invitation to the counter-elite, the coming Aristocrats, to decide for themselves their relation toward this movement called transhumanism and whether it will gain their endorsement or resistance.

Let me make my position perfectly clear: Negative selection of therapies and modalities is not transhumanism; positive selection is. I resist transhumanism in all of its manifestations. I would rather live an imperfect life of suffering and uncertainty in an imperfect world as a real human man unfolding at the speed of nature than live a "perfect" life in a "perfect" world governed by the opinions of cyberneticists, hedonists and sociologists unfolding at the speed of technics.

XII

<u>Fragmentation as Purification</u>

There are many who lament fragmentation thinking it is a form of failure. Unaware of the principles of cyclical time and Cultural Vitalism or preferring not to believe them, they refuse the advent of the terminus of their great society wanting it instead to remain and continue forever. All civilizations eventually come to an end, but the people live on to create anew even though it may be many centuries before recentralization and imperium can be newly established under the auspices of an advanced people.

There are great benefits to fragmentation that are represented in the microcosm of the alchemical process of *solve et coagula.* Dissolving and coming back together – dividing and reconstituting – allows for the parts of the whole to be purified in their divided, discrete state. When parts are fully combined into an integrated complex whole, there is far too much mutual dependency for any of those parts to independently purify and strengthen itself without catastrophically altering the whole. One small change somewhere in the system can have a domino effect which can damage the entire system. But should those parts be divided one from another and made relatively self-sufficient, fundamental changes can be made to a single part with only moderate effects on the whole.

This is also true for the negative. Should one part of an integrated whole become infected with disease, the entire system will suffer. Should divided parts fall victim to some disease, the other parts can isolate themselves with relative ease and remain healthy.

In political terms: social engineers and conspirators love large centralized authorities. A single central government ruled by a tiny number of the governing elite is much easier to influence and control than hundreds of small polities, each with its own governing elite, ideology, economic system, body of laws, and customs. A conspiracy only needs a handful of well-placed operators to pull the levers of power within the United States federal government having coerced only a tiny number of politicians and businessmen, but should that government cease to govern and the country fragment into dozens or even hundreds of smaller independent polities, it would be very easy to defend against criminality, corruption and coercion. A conspiracy would now require many more thousands of operators to influence these small polities and their organization would be orders of magnitude more difficult to maintain.

Small polities can watch for corruption much more easily in much the same way that citizens of a small town quickly and easily discover who is responsible for a recent crime. It is also easier to pass anti-corruption laws and other sensible self-defense measures in small polities, as the citizens thereof would likely be on the same page, or very close to it, ideologically, politically and economically. If a local government wanted to, say, ban a particular group of people from holding any position in politics, business, education, and so on, it would be quite a trivial thing to pass such a law. Most countries and small polities have had such laws for millennia. Any attempt to do so on a large scale in a large polity already under the entrenched influence of social engineers would be met with derision and cries of injustice and would be essentially impossible.

Remigration laws are also easier to pass and the logistics of remigration become very easy on a continent of small polities. Regions which possess unwelcome groups of people can move such people into the regions where they might be welcomed now that there is a multi-polar plurality of ideologies and cultures within a single continent. Europe after the Second World War saw the remigration of tens of millions of Europeans and non-Europeans into their respective homelands. Germans were taken from everywhere in the world and placed in Germany. English were taken from everywhere in the world and placed in England. Italians were taken from everywhere and placed in Italy. Russians were taken from everywhere and placed in Russia and so on. Every European country and some non-European ones had their respective diasporas returned to themselves in less than five years. It was logistically simple, legally sound, and the bureaucracy was quite efficient. Anyone who argues that remigration is too difficult or even impossible clearly has not studied the history of 20th Century Europe or the histories of other fragmented societies.

Fragmentation allows for the creation of new dynasties and new elite groups as people are freed from the constraints, pressures, roadblocks, sabotage, and repression that they suffer under a corrupt central authority. Many people who have "failed" in conventional life due to the political and economic machinations of selfish and evil people and the broken systems in place but have secured good reputations for themselves locally will see their success rapidly appear as their friends, family and neighbors would happily support, employ and follow them. Having proved their skill and virtue in their daily lives with those who know them and live near them, the sabotage carried out by the corrupt elite who can operate impersonally from vast distances due to the ease of influencing a central authority would no longer be an obstacle if that central authority ceased to exercise any power or have any sovereignty. The corrupt elite would immediately lose their foothold over our society and the counter-elite would almost instantaneously rise to power and prominence to the great relief of the localities benefitting from the counter-elite surge.

The reclamation of land and resources is also made easier. If large corporations who control enormous swathes of land for their deleterious agricultural and industrial operations no longer receive their privileged protections from government and police, locals would be able to claim that land for themselves for better or worse. Likely for the better seeing as most of this land is wasted on useless and harmful crops like corn and soybeans and is polluted by technological industrial processes. Virtually any other usage would be an improvement. Even if some of the same uses remained, they would occur on smaller scales seeing that many polities would be competing for these parcels of land and the large corporations would be bereft of their legal protections and would themselves fragment abandoning their capacity to exploit resources on large scales.

And finally, the dissolution of the North Atlantic Treaty Organization and the hegemonic ambitions of the United States and the European Union will allow the world to be envisioned not along ideological lines, but along ethnic lines. The politics of the future are not geopolitics or corporate policy but ethnopolitics.

All white nations are facing decline and initiating renaissance. White identitarian forces are much stronger in Russia than in the rest of the white world where such ideas are considered "dangerous" and are repressed by self-hating liberals and non-white invaders. The Russian youth are far more vital and resistant to liberal corruption than Westerners and so they have the responsibility of leading a new alliance with the entire white world from Ireland to Vladivostok to America. The dissolution of the corrupt Western governments and institutions that work against the interests of white people would mean the liberation of the ethnic spiritual forces of the Russian people and unleashing them as the central unifying factor of reconquest and revolution that will awaken the white world to its true identity and unity.

***

In short, do not waste time and energy lamenting or attempting to restore that which is dead or dying. Such conservatism is a pathetic weakness and shows a lack of vision and force. Focus instead on preserving yourself and your people first and foremost. After that, the establishment of new economic systems and cultural forms will come more naturally.

Leave some flowers in the graveyard of the West, but cast your eyes toward the horizon.

XIII

<u>Cycles, Spirals and Lines</u>

Perhaps in the transcendent eternity of the Absolute, time is not experienced and is of little importance, but down here in the muck of the mortal world, Chronos produces and devours his offspring. Time is the soil in which the seeds of our souls grow and develop – the chrysalis in which our spirit discovers and constitutes its true shape. It is the battleground on which we fight, the stage on which we dance, the field on which we sow and reap. The passage of time is arguably the single most important aspect of the earthbound human experience. How one perceives this passage will determine most of the fundamental attitudes, beliefs and behaviors a person exhibits throughout their mortal life.

Should one view time in a linear fashion as having a beginning at a starting point in the past and extending into the infinite future, they will likely profess beliefs in progress, evolution and modern astrophysical hypotheses. In the cultural and political sense, they may very well consider the present to be better than the past and the future to be better than the present. They will consider all societies which came before them to be inferior antecedents and stepping stones to their present greatness and that humanity is "working toward a brighter tomorrow" where all benefactions will increase and detriments decrease within the human condition. The great civilizations of the past were nothing more than learning experiences – failed experiments. It is a worldview of incremental messianism in which a future utopia slowly unfolds as intellect increases, superstition decreases, political values are liberalized and technologies advance to solve more and more human problems and deficiencies. It is an attitude fueled by incessant and perpetual hope dangling in front of one's face like a carrot on stick. Entire populations are lured along the path, industriously toiling to achieve this brighter tomorrow in all fields of human endeavor, never quite being able to eat the carrot, but dreaming of the day when they might sink their teeth into its glorious promise of salvation. Always believing that nothing is ever good enough and must be improved, their secondary fuel, the reverse seal of hope, is constant dissatisfaction. Ashamed of their ancestors for being illiberal, ignorant barbarians, they wish to put as much distance between those savages and themselves as possible, to sprint down the highway of time to a distant future where they may forget these embarrassing chapters of history and revel in the warm glow of "how far we've come." And fear is their constant companion – fear of death, of an untimely or accidental conclusion to their great project of the future. So much hope and desire is placed on the achievement of some envisioned future that they run and hide from death, deny its existence, speak of it only in hushed tones, in somber regret-filled ceremonies, or not at all. It is considered a morbid topic of discussion, distasteful and rude. One who accepts death as natural and is fearless of it is thought to be a lunatic, a madman, a great offender of polite society and all that is dignified. It is a cultural *faux pas* to speak calmly and contentedly about this future inevitability. It shocks the listener into the bitter realization that all things end – that their Great Society Project may very easily fail with a single mishap and that their individual self is bound for the grave and all their enjoyments of life, their hopes and dreams of constant satisfaction of their ceaseless desires will one day come to a conclusion. This fear sets them on the path of obsession for immortality.

Should one view time as cyclical, having neither a beginning nor an end, or rather constantly oscillating between beginnings and endings, one will have a very different experience of reality and set of beliefs, attitudes and behaviors. They will have a seasonal outlook on events. The rise of a civilization will be recognized as the season of spring when its population booms and its youthful enthusiasm stakes its claim, and when it has reached its fullness of learning, science, religion, war, art, and self-expression, it will be in its summer. As advancements slow down and a culture begins to withdraw inwardly, seeing less importance in external expansions and expressions, it will have entered its autumn, and after this period when its great epochs are but a distant memory and its people are unrecognizable from those of their vibrant youthful eras, when reminiscence takes up more time than new activity, the winter will have set in. Each culture is a full expression unto itself, lacking nothing, leading nowhere but to its own fulfillment and death, progressing for no great future, but simply experiencing existence and being like a garden that is planted, grows, blooms, and perishes. Perhaps the greatest ripest fruits will be plucked for a higher transcendent destiny beyond the reach of Chronos and his compost bin. Considering oneself as neither better nor worse than those who came before or those who will come after, all that is hoped for is to be the best expression of their vine – the sweetest grape, the juiciest peach, the heartiest potato, the straightest oak, the broadest mushroom – before the coming of winter. Unperturbed by progressive thinking and future dreaming and the dissatisfaction this foments, contentment is much easier to cultivate when one knows that all things die eventually. When death is not a thing to be feared, when endings are known to be inevitable, it is easier to accept and plan for new beginnings which will occur absent of one's presence. The world continues after we die, after we are forgotten. It renews itself constantly and moves on to new and different expressions. One's only worry in old age is wondering if they depleted the soil or enriched it for the next harvest.

There is a third view which pretends to a compromise between the linear and cyclical. It is the spiral view of time; the view in which history does not repeat, but it certainly rhymes. It considers that current and future cultures learn from the past. Although each culture lives and dies like an organism, they may exceed those who came before by observation, avoiding their mistakes and attempting to carry on their successes – standing on their shoulders. While indeed the great civilizations may go through their seasons from spring to winter, birth to death, each does so in an expanded and improved manner. This, in my view, is fundamentally the linear-progressive-evolutionary view of the passage of time only slightly modified with the superficial aspects of the cyclical. It does not fully embrace the attitude of the cyclical but it does fully embrace the attitude of the linear. The incessant hope, dissatisfaction and fear are still very much in the ascendent while the contentment and seasonal wisdom of the cyclical view are found only in rare personalities or those who have lived to an extreme age. So difficult it is to free oneself from the dominant "truth system[15]" of a given era that even alternative theories are not alternative at all.

With roughly only eight thousand years of recorded history, it is my view that the linear theory does not have nearly enough evidence to be proven true. If homo sapiens sapiens has existed on the conservative side of theoretical anthropology for thirty thousand years or according to the more current theory for up to four million years, or even a hundred million years, then eight thousand years is not a long enough timeline to make many meaningful observations. Homo sapiens sapiens may have achieved technological civilizations many times which have come to an end and were entirely forgotten. If we have had these brains and bodies for millions of years, then the ancient Egyptians could have built rocket ships and computers had they the urge. They simply did not want to. They had other goals and dreams like how to properly navigate the underworld after death. Technological advancement is merely the daydream of modern man, more precisely of Anglo-Saxon man. It may not be a mark of progress at all but simply the expression of a particular great civilization which will one day cease to express itself.

From a practical standpoint, it is arguably better to operate from the cyclical view whether it is factually true or not. In this mode of conduct, we carry out actions and behaviors which we know are fruitful and beneficial on cultural, political, social, spiritual and economic levels. We know what is tried and true, we see the repeatable results, and we stick to it; we "play it safe," and we prepare for the next season recognizing the changes and transitions as they arise. In other words: there is no need to reinvent the wheel or fix what is not broken. The linear view places hope in novel theories that may cause either benefit or detriment. It is experimental and unknown whether changes in technology, pedagogy, politics or culture will bear nutritious fruit or poison the well. It may also cause people to imagine problems where none truly exist by incessantly believing that everything can be improved. This attitude can encourage the thought that nearly every single thing about life is currently wrong and needs improvement. They may view minor inconveniences or natural limitations as utter injustices and fundamental problems that must be eradicated. An obsession with solving problems generally creates many more new problems anyway and net quality of life stays precisely the same. Perhaps people succumbed to infections and saber tooth tiger attacks in the past, but at least the water was clean, work was light, and there were no obscenely loud airplanes tearing through the sky overhead. Which world is really better? Are these two worlds really all that different? How does one define quality of life?

***

There is a view that, depending on your theoretical needs, cuts through all three, combines all three or ignores all three to an extent and produces its own framework. This is Sorokin's Truth Systems cycle. All cultures move through various phases: the ideational springtime, the idealistic early summer, the active sensate late summer, the passive sensate autumn, and the cynical sensate early winter which leads to the crisis of late winter and a transition to a new ideational beginning when the cycle restarts[15].

The ideational phase is characterized by new systems of perception, epistemology, philosophy and ontology irrupting from the minds of great individuals. The idealistic phase is when these systems become peared down and the favorites institutionalized and systematized to form the scaffold of a civilization. The active sensate phase is when skepticism of these earlier ideas sets in and their spiritual quality is seen as unimportant precipitating a shift to materialistic consciousness and exploration of the outer world. The passive sensate phase occurs when these materialistic hypotheses are believed quite seriously like religious dogma. The cynical sensate phase is when this materialistic dogma destroys meaning and fulfillment in people's lives resulting in hedonism, nihilism, and corruption. This inculcates a crisis phase in which there is great need for a new ideational phase.

Sorokin himself subscribed to the spiral view of the passage of time believing that no civilization truly collapses but comes to near collapse, or low points, during crises and always renews in one way or another. He views the modern West as being an echo and continuation of ancient Rome. This earned him the ire of his contemporaries who either doggedly adhered to the linear dogma or wanted to separate themselves from past cultures and believed themselves to have nothing in common whatsoever with them. Make of that what you will.

***

It is my view that during the crisis phase, the great prophets and heroes of the next culture (or the next arc of the spiral, depending on your view) arise. These great individuals create the systems of thought and action which form the foundation and lifeblood of the coming ethnos. They found spiritual traditions, military orders, Aristocratic initiation methods, pedagogy, economic systems, and all the other things that a cultural Oversoul needs from its beginning to express itself fully throughout its lifespan.

These great individuals do not concern themselves with preserving the forms of their parent culture. They do not sit and lament in the graveyard of their ancestors crying over the crumbled monuments and corrupted institutions of their collapsing civilization. They do not pore through necromantic manuals attempting to learn the secrets of resurrection in order to bring false life into the corpse of what has already fulfilled itself. They honor and respect what came before them, they learn what they must from it, they mourn for a while if they have to, but they know that what has died shall remain dead. They collect themselves, look toward the future and act to bring it about.

These false traditionalists desperately trying to maintain the relevance of their church, these conservatives merely attempting to conserve a slightly earlier form of liberalism, these right wingers waving the banners and shouting the slogans of ghosts, these pagans defaulting to atavistic ritual and precepts – they are all like the pathetic hipsters who listen to vinyl records and pine for the days when grandma would bake them endless sheets of cookies and mom was always home and dad would play catch with them. There is nothing Traditionalistic about the Church of Waiting Forever. There is nothing Traditional written in the Constitution. The reactionary movements of the first half of the Twentieth Century were merely baby steps in the right direction. The old pagan gods are sleeping, transformed or dead. And there was nothing Traditionalistic about the 1950's.

Do not ally yourself with the past. Being nostalgic for a time you never experienced or for a time that has come to an end is a repulsive weakness. It is the desire to crawl back into your mother's womb and refuse to be a man. Your church has failed. Move on. Your government and its attendant ideology has failed. Move on. The previous movements have failed. Move on. The old gods are uninterested. Move on. The "good old days" are but a dream. Move on. You cannot restore what is dead, nor should you. There are new expressions and forms lying latent *in potentia* that need you to recognize them and act so they may manifest in our world. There are new temples that God wants built. There are new constitutions which must be written. There are new borders to be drawn. Respect and honor what has died to the extent that it is reverential and necessary *in memorium*, but no more than that. Your parents want you to live your own life. The dead and dying Oversouls want to see what you will create, how you will live, what you will achieve. They do not need you to act out a hollow charade of what they once were. They demand uniqueness and variety in the types of cultures which form around the nucleus of the earth and from the imaginations of your people.

You do not need to imitate anything if you listen to the innermost callings of your spirit. You should be nothing other than totally and completely yourself.

Bibliography

1. Pobedonostsev, Konstantin. *Reflections of a Russian Statesmen.* 1898. Translator: Richards, Grant. Imperium Press.
2. Maxwell, Mike. *Tribal Future of the West.* 2025. Imperium Press.
3. *The Agni Purana.* Editor: J.L. Shastri. 1954. Motilal Banarsidass.
4. Yockey, Francis P. *Imperium.* 1948. Invictus Books. 2011.
5. Turchin, Peter. *End Times: Elites, Counter-Elites, and the Path of Political Disintegration.* 2023. Penguin Press.
6. Lao Tzu. *Tao te Ching.* 1961. St. John's University Press, New York.
7. Spengler, Oswald. 1926. *The Decline of the West.* Knopf, Alfred A.
8. Jung, Carl G. *Memories, Dreams, Reflections.* 1989. Vintage.
9. Boas, Franz. *Anthropology and Modern Life.* 1987. Dover Publications.
10. Gravlee, Clarence. Presentation: *Race, Biology, and Culture: Rethinking the Connections.* 2013. University of Oregon Department of Anthropology.
11. Sheldrake, Rupert. *A New Science of Life: The Hypothesis of Morphic Resonance.* 1995. Park Street Press

12. Goethe, Johann W. *The Metamorphosis of Plants.* 2009. Massachusetts Institute of Technology Press.

13. Steiner, Rudolf. Lecture: *Man as Symphony of the Creative Word Part Four: The Secrets of the Human Organism: GA 230.* 11 November 1923. Dornach, Switzerland. Rsarchive.org/Lectures/ManSymphony/19231111p01.html

14. Dugin, Alexander. *Ethnosociology.* 2019. Arktos.

15. Sorokin, Pitirim. *Social and Cultural Dynamics.* 1991. Transaction Publishers.

16. Loxbo, K. (2018). *Ethnic diversity, out-group contacts and social trust in a high-trust society.* Acta Sociologica, 61(2), 182-201.

17. Abascal, Maria. Baldassarri, Delia. *Love Thy Neighbor? Ethnoracial Diversity and Trust Reexamined.* American Journal of Sociology, Vol. 121 #3, November 2015. University of Chicago.

18. Shaw, Clifford R. McKay, Henry D. *Juvenile Delinquency in Urban Areas.* 1969. University of Chicago.

19. Tyler, Tom R. *Why People Obey the Law.* 2006. Yale University.

20. Auken, Ida. 2016. World Economic Forum. https://medium.com/world-economic-forum/welcome-to-2030-

iown-nothing-have-no-privacy-and-life-has-never-been-better-ee2eed62f710

21. United States of America Department of Homeland Security. 2026. https://www.dhs.gov/behavioral-threat-assessment-and-management

22. Bolton, Kerry. *The Perversion of Normality: From the Marquis de Sade to Cyborgs.* Arktos. 2021.